ALL HOLY MEN AND WOMEN

ALL HOLY MEN AND WOMEN

A Paulist Litany of Saints

EDITED BY
Thomas A. Kane, CSP

Paulist Press
New York / Mahwah, NJ

Illustrated by Frank Sabatté, CSP

Cover image by Daniela Illing / Shutterstock.com
Cover and book design by Lynn Else

Library of Congress Control Number: 2014933444

ISBN 978-0-8091-4863-9 (paperback)
ISBN 978-1-58768-353-4 (e-book)

Published by Paulist Press
997 Macarthur Boulevard
Mahwah, New Jersey 07430

www.paulistpress.com

Printed and bound in the
United States of America

In memory of Stan MacNevin, CSP, companion and mentor.

This collection is dedicated to my friends at
the St. Thomas More Newman Center
at the Ohio State University, Columbus, Ohio,
and to the Paulist Associates, all holy women and men.

CONTENTS

CONTENTS

CONTENTS

CONTENTS

INTRODUCTION

Saints have always fascinated and delighted me. When I was growing up, I collected saint cards. Not quite as large or as flashy as baseball cards, these colorful cards had a drawing of the saint on the front with a short biography and prayer on the back. Our local religious goods store near the parish church had a revolving rack of these saints on display, and I was one of their best customers. At school, we would often share our cards with our classmates or trade cards to see which saint had the most arresting story. In the group were priests, nuns, popes, bishops, even martyrs, with a few layfolk who made it on the official list. Even at my young age, I was surprised at how top heavy this list was with clerics, because there are so many fervent lay people, who can also be inspirational!

While the painted images may have been a bit saccharine, these models of the faith were not sugarcoated. The stories spoke of courage, devotion, following Christ to foreign lands and enduring hardship, torture, even death. To young eyes, the saints were heroes, and we so aspired to be like these saints!

To this day, I continue invoking the saints. My friends often think I am crazed when I prayerfully petition my beloved St. Anthony to assist me, as I drive around Boston in search of the elusive on-street parking place. What may begin as skepticism on the part of my passengers slowly turns to faint credibility, when a parking space suddenly appears. It happens with great frequency, I might add. I smile and thank St. Anthony for his marvelous care for my *machini*. Anthony of Padua, though Portuguese by birth, prefers direct address in Italian! It's all part of the ritual. But can we really expect the saints to be on call? Of course not! As we continue to uncover their spiritual insights, we may find ourselves inspired to lead lives of loving service.

In recent years, I have been wanting to collect the saints again, not in a pack of cards this time, but something more substantive, something to connect these holy women and men to our modern life. As I was researching the patron saints of my community, the Paulist Fathers, it struck me that a collection of reflections about these holy men and women would be a perfect project.

As I began compiling the official list of Paulist patronal saints, I decided to open the collection to other holy men and women whose lives both inspire us in the twenty-first century and can also be ever-present models in our faith journey. These are women and men who embody the charism of the Paulist Fathers: fervor for evangelization, the healing presence of reconciliation, sensitivity to social justice, and an all-embracing view of ecumenism and interreligious dialogue.

To illustrate the collection, I invited Frank Sabatté, a Paulist artist and sculptor to capture the special qualities of each saint in pen and ink. I then began asking friends and colleagues to see if they would join me in this writing venture. It was exciting to read their reflections and muse on the value and relevance of these holy ones for today. The project rekindled my boyhood love for the saints, and I feel honored to share this saintly group with a wider audience.

This litany spans two thousand years of history, covers many continents, including women and men from every walk of life. Most are officially canonized, some are in process, and some are considered "holy" role models.

Most saints have specially designated feast days, associated with a specific day of the year. These feast days first arose from the very early Christian custom of the annual commemoration of martyrs on the dates of their deaths, at the same time celebrating their birth into heaven. Many saints' feasts are celebrated on the day of their death or martyrdom.

Saints are also patrons—of professions, cities, countries, and even religious communities, usually reflecting the specific mission and goals of that group. Since our founder, Isaac Thomas Hecker, began ministry as a Redemptorist priest in New York City, many saints on his original Paulist list were taken over from our brother Redemptorists, who share a missionary spirit and are engaged in the ministries of preaching, evangelizing and healing.

The saints often represent many different virtues or attributes, and it is not always easy to box them neatly into categories. Here is an overview of the collection:

- Mary of Magdala, Paul, Patrick, Alphonsus Liguori, Francis de Sales, Isaac Jogues, and Isaac Thomas Hecker: evangelizing forces, spreading the gospel of Jesus Christ.
- Francis of Assisi, Philip Neri, John Henry Cardinal Newman, and Pope John XXIII: seeking to reform and rebuild the Church.
- Elizabeth Ann Seton, Dietrich Bonhoeffer, Martin Luther King, Jr., Dorothy Day, and Archbishop Oscar Romero: working for peace and social justice.
- Mary of Nazareth, The Virgin of Guadalupe: being the loving mother of us all.
- Joseph: reaching out to workers in a quiet way.
- Hildegard of Bingen, Thomas Aquinas, Ignatius Loyola, Teresa of Avila, and John of the Cross: bringing theological vigor and spiritual insight to the Church.

Our Paulist founder, Isaac Thomas Hecker, understood holiness very well, and he compared the saints' lives to folly:

> To become holy we must become fools; fools for the sake of Jesus Christ....The folly of the saints was a divine intoxication. Without this folly certain saints would never have fulfilled the designs of God in regard to them. In order to become holy, we must suffer contempt or persecution and sometimes both....One, who

> would conceal a valuable treasure from being discovered and stolen, must make use of a chest so much the less costly as his treasure is valuable. This is the secret of the folly of the saints. There is no other way to mortify our pride, vanity or ambition or of subjugating our reason to the divine light of faith. Jesus gave us the example: he was counted as a fool. Oh, the wisdom of the folly of the saints! (unpublished spiritual notebook, 1854)

I want to thank the many authors, who so graciously contributed to this collection, for their insights and affection for the saints. A special thanks to Mark-David Janus and Donna Crilly at Paulist Press for their encouragement to do this project; to Suzanne Beebe, who composed some of the new prayers; to Paul Robichaud, our Paulist historian; to Frank Desiderio, editor of the *Paulist Prayer Book*; to Patricia Watson, my ever-watchful copy editor; to the Sisters of Charity, New York; and to the Baltimore Province of the Redemptorists.

I trust you will enjoy reading this volume, find solace in the various lives presented and rejoice in a true communion of saints.

Thomas A. Kane, CSP
Autumn 2013
Chestnut Hill, Massachusetts

Elizabeth Ann Seton

(1774–1821)

January 4

Elizabeth Ann Seton was born in New York City, one of two daughters of a prominent Episcopal family on August 28, 1774. As she matured, she was a popular guest at parties and balls. She married William Magee Seton in 1794, and they had five children. With the death of his father, their fortunes declined.

Elizabeth was involved in social work and co-founded the Society for the Relief of Poor Widows with Children in 1797, and she became known as the "Protestant Sister of Charity." Her husband died in 1803 in Italy, and the family was left bankrupt by her husband's failed business and ill health. While waiting to return to America, Elizabeth was drawn to the Catholic faith and Eucharist. She converted to Catholicism in 1805, which alienated her from her extended family. To support her children, she established a boarding school and took on various jobs to supplement her income. When her sister-in-law, Cecelia Seton, became a Roman Catholic, Elizabeth's angry supporters withdrew.

Hearing of her need, William DuBourg, a Sulpician, invited her to Baltimore in 1808 to open the first free Catholic school for girls; this became the basis for the Catholic parochial system in the United States. In 1809, Elizabeth made her vows before Bishop John Carroll of Baltimore and established the Sisters of Charity of St. Joseph, the first American religious society, devoted to teaching and serving the poor. For special occasions the sisters wore black dresses with shoulder capes, with a simple white bonnet tied under the chin.

In 1811, Mother Seton adopted with some modifications the rules and constitution of St. Vincent de Paul, and the institute, sanctioned by ecclesiastical authority, became a religious order. Afterward a residence for the Sisters, a novitiate, a boarding school for young girls, a school for poor children, and an orphan asylum were built. In time, the order spread throughout the Northeast. At her death there were more than twenty communities of Sisters of Charity, conducting free schools, orphanages, boarding schools, and hospitals in Pennsylvania, New York, Ohio, Delaware, Massachusetts, Virginia, Missouri, and Louisiana, and the District of Columbia. Mother Seton died of tuberculosis in 1821.

The life of Elizabeth Ann Seton spans the full spectrum of human experience. She was a New York socialite, a devoted wife, a dedicated volunteer in charitable organizations, the mother of five children, a convert to Roman Catholicism, an educator, friend of the poor, catechist, and a tireless servant of God. She was beatified by Pope John XXIII and canonized the first American-born saint by Pope Paul VI in 1975. She is the patron saint of loss of children and of widows. Her feast day is January 4.

ELIZABETH ANN SETON

An Example of "Holy Dexterity"

Colleen M. Griffith

There is an art to good juggling. It requires skill and grace, and a capacity to handle multiple things at once. Observing talented jugglers can be mesmerizing. They are not thrown off by changes in the speed, motion, or number of items in the air. The concentration they bring to their craft is remarkable, as is their extraordinary dexterity.

People today find themselves having to juggle multiple responsibilities as a result of a commitment to plural vocations, rising from seen and unforeseen life circumstances. A painter, sensing a genuine calling to her art, finds herself caring for two aging parents, while needing a further job to make ends meet. An inner city teacher, believing fully in the power of education, discovers himself being asked to help his students and families outside of class time, even as he tries to complete his Master's degree in Educational Leadership at the local university. A husband and father dies of a rare disease, leaving a widow, a single mother of three, in need of full-time work to support a young family.

Life continues to roll, and new responsibilities emerge. Our vocational choices require plenty of tending, as do unexpected events that signal the need for additional commitments on our part, giving us still more to juggle. Active juggling of multiple responsibilities and commitments is not for the faint-hearted. It takes focus, energy, and practical wisdom. One has to discern what is necessary to keep in play and what is not. And sometimes the things we thought were ours to juggle are not the things we've got to play with anymore at all. Suppleness, a holy dexterity, becomes the virtue for which we hope.

A prominent figure from the historic Catholic Christian tradition who demonstrates an abundance of "holy dexterity" in juggling multiple and diverse responsibilities is the American saint, Elizabeth Ann Baxley Seton (1774–1821). Born in New York City, this wife, mother, educator, administrator, foundress, and community superior was left to raise five children under the age of seven following the death of her husband. She looked after her husband's orphaned younger brothers and sisters, regularly assisted the dying as a ministry she held sacred, established the first American women's religious community, and became the founding mother of the Catholic School system in the United States. Over the course of her lifetime, she knew affluence and poverty, love and loss, the fullness of spiritual consolation and the depths of sorrow. Faced with great obstacles and dire hardships, she approached the challenges that beset her with creative fidelity, prayerfully reassessing her path at every crossroad, opting for what she deemed most practically wise. Ever fired by her deep Christian faith, she would jump in with both feet in response to new directions that needed taking, doing so with a positive spirit that attracted others, enlivening many a jaded soul. For these many reasons, Elizabeth Seton stands as a powerful symbol for millions of contemporary un-canonized saints who daily assume complex responsibilities with courage, refusing to "drop the ball" when forced to juggle multiple and necessary commitments.

Seton's husband died when she was twenty-nine years old, leaving her to raise three daughters and two sons as a single mother. As a married woman, inspired by the work of St. Vincent de Paul, she had organized a group of women who regularly visited the sick in their homes. Now, trying to support herself as a widow and her children, she turned her energies to teaching, beginning a small school with four boarding students and her own three daughters.

Raised an Episcopalian, Seton's introduction to Catholicism began following her husband's death. When Seton's husband became seriously ill, the two went to Italy with their oldest daughter hoping that the warmer climate would help him rally. Upon arrival, however, they were held in quarantine, during which time her beloved William died. The families of William's business associates looked after Elizabeth and her daughter, welcoming them with caring and heartfelt hospitality. It was through their influence that Elizabeth Seton was introduced to Roman Catholicism, and soon thereafter she became a Catholic. This decision evoked the chagrin of many family members and friends. Her Catholicism posed difficulties for her professionally as well, in a dominantly Protestant New York where parents feared the influence of Catholicism on their children's minds. When news of Seton's conversion to Catholicism broke, many families removed their daughters from her school.

During this period of ostracism, Seton received an unusual invitation from William DuBourg, a Sulpician bishop, to begin a Catholic community school. Following her best lights, in accord with her own natural proclivity for prayer and an apostolic spirituality, she moved to Emmitsburg, Maryland, where she established Saint Joseph's Academy and Free School, dedicated to the education of young women. This became the first parochial school for girls in the United States. Juggling the demands of teaching, administration, and parenting, she went on to found a religious community in Emmitsburg, a community of women committed to the care of the children of the poor. The group initially was called the Sisters of Charity of Saint Joseph, later simply the Sisters of Charity, and Elizabeth Seton became "Mother Seton."[1]

Over the years, Seton faced many challenges. She experienced bouts of personal poor health and troubling financial concerns. She found herself in the agonizing position of repeatedly being the one to accompany loved ones through death, not only her husband William and her father; but her sister-in-law and best friend, Rebecca Seton; two of her own beloved daughters; several friends; and younger sisters in community. Throughout it all, she remained a person of prayer, who embraced contradictions with hopeful realism, and sought to keep her faith concrete and practical. The suppleness of spirit that she developed over the course of her lifetime blossomed into a saintly dexterity, one utterly real and grounded in God.

In her writings and in accounts of her spiritual life, specific practices of Elizabeth stand out as suggestive for contemporary people of faith who juggle multiple responsibilities. These include (1) a commitment to practical enactment of love of God and neighbor in whatever circumstances one finds oneself; (2) the adoption of a "can do" mentality, grounded in the realization that the work at hand is God's work; (3) prioritization of what is truly important in any given situation and fidelity to it; and (4) regular practice of prayerful praise to God, particularly when tired, lacking in cheer, or worn out. These practices helped Elizabeth Seton to maintain her balance and to juggle wisely without being overwhelmed, and they continue to inspire contemporary women and men interested in a way of holy dexterity today.

A Practical Love of God: Seton focused on what the embodiment of love of God and neighbor for the sake of the Reign of God looked like amidst changing life contexts and shifts in roles. When she had the wrenching experience of losing her husband and becoming a widow at a young age, she turned around and founded the Society for the Relief of Poor Widows. In Seton's view, the experiences we undergo point us in the direction of the love of God and neighbor in fresh ways. Her sincerity and conviction coupled with her attraction to a charity that was eminently practical led others to follow her. Speaking to her sisters in community later in her life, she proclaimed: "Sisters of Charity! Your admirable name must excite in you every preparation to do justice to your vocation."[2] The vocation of loving effectively in ways that were concretely useful to others became the central commitment of multiple branches of the Sisters of Charity. Generations of sisters and laypersons who look to Elizabeth Seton as foundress and sister in faith, continue to underscore the importance of embodying a practical charity through peace work and immigration reform, education and social welfare, ministry in schools and colleges, orphanages and asylums, hospitals and nursing centers.

A "Can Do" Attitude by God's Grace: A second practice apparent in the life of Elizabeth Seton was her adoption of a positive, "can do" mentality. The basis for this attitudinal disposition came not from an overassessment of her own capacities and purposes, but rather from a deep conviction that the work at hand was one piece of something much bigger than her, namely the work of God as sustained by the grace of God. Seton continually showed healthy detachment from her own efforts; she wrote: "If I succeed, I bless God. If I do not succeed I bless God, for then it shall be right that I not succeed."[3] She would leverage her resources and lead in innovative directions without being overly concerned about success, because the work itself was God's. If the work wasn't of God, it would fail, and that, in her mind, would be as it should be.

Knowing What Is Most Important: As part of her practical approach to work, Seton regularly prioritized what was ultimately most important in any situation, and then stayed faithful to it. She understood discernment of priorities to be essential, because for her, that which we prioritize before God, becomes "our duty." She observes, "We must learn what our duty is, pray to Him for the grace to do it, and then set our whole heart and soul to perform it."[4] In her own life, when it appeared that Seton might have to leave the community that she had founded because having children to care for did not fit the mold of existing religious orders, she stood faithful to what she identified as her primary vocation, that of being a mother, naming her children as her first priority. The complexity of this particular situation got resolved through an exercise of good communal dexterity and imagination. The newly formed American community opted for independence from their European model, thereby making exceptions to the usual rules.

Seton was able to include her children and the care of them in her life as a vowed religious.

A further illustration is helpful. Because Elizabeth Seton's new community became associated with the Daughters of Charity that Vincent de Paul established two centuries earlier in France, plans were made for some sisters from France to visit Emmitsburg to help construct the new foundation. When this plan ran amuck, due to Emperor Napoleon's refusal to let the French sisters leave, Seton prioritized timely spiritual formation of her American sisters and undertook the work of interpreting the Rule of St. Vincent de Paul for her sisters herself, thereby educating a young American community in the spirit of Vincent de Paul.

A Practice of Prayerful Praise: A fourth practice prominent in the life of Elizabeth Seton is intentional *praise* of God, a cherished way of prayer that she sensed bolstered cheerfulness of spirit in herself, enabling her to be more adroit at handling complex life realities. "Praise the Lord, O my soul," she exclaims. "Praise Him that the blessed impulse of grace may rebound to your own happiness and glory for to Him, your praise can add nothing; to yourself, it is now the means of grace and comfort, and hereafter will be your pleasure and joy through eternity."[5] Prayers of praise lent perspective, and reminded Seton of her confidence in God as Guide: "With such a Guide, can I fear; with such a Friend, shall I not be satisfied; with such a Supporter, can I fail?"[6] Songs of praise to God spared her of "the pain, both of retrospection and anticipation,"[7] making it more possible to "correspond to the grace of the moment"[8] and freeing her to place trust in the lead of God's creative spirit. A practice of praise remained central to Seton's spirituality throughout her life. It corresponded with an ardent desire in her: "While I live, while I have my being, in time and through eternity, let me praise my God."[9]

Concrete enactment of the great command to love, a practical approach to work as ultimately God's, discernment of what is most important amongst competing goods, and a habit of praise of God all stand as hallmarks of the life and way of Elizabeth Seton.

Cumulatively considered, these practices become pointers for us, ushering in the possibility of deft leadership on our part too, and hope for a holy dexterity as we juggle multiple life responsibilities. Looking to Elizabeth Seton as a companion in faith, we pray, "*Presente!*[10] *Be with us as guide and mentor, as we seek to respond to the practical graces inherent in plural vocations and unforeseen life circumstances.*"

MAGNIFICAT OF ELIZABETH ANN SETON[11]

(Italicized words are Elizabeth's own.)

While I live, while I have my being, I will sing praises to my God;
For God has looked with love on my *simple and confiding* heart;
generations to come will call me *Mother of many daughters.*
For the One who alone is mighty
    has changed my *poverty and sorrow*
into the power to do great things. Holy is God's name!
In every age *our sweet Providence*
    has continually showered *mercy over us.*
God, my defense and shield and strength and Salvation,
    confuses the proud of heart,
casts the mighty from their thrones,
    and calls the lowly *to look up with hope.*
God *raises me from the dust to feel that I am near* the Light,
and *drives away all terrors to fill me with* peace.
God's abundance fills the hungry,
while the rich are sent away empty-handed.
God, my Shepherd, sustains me in faith, hope, and charity
and leads me *to assist the poor* with tender compassion.
The God who remembers, who *never slumbers or sleeps,*
upheld our mothers and fathers, our ancestors in faith.
So too for us and for our children, God keeps the promise,
Mercy for the future, as sure as the past.

Glory be to the Father, and to the Son,
and to the Holy Spirit, one God, forever and ever. Amen.

NOTES

1. A detailed biographical sketch of Elizabeth Seton's life and work is provided by Annabelle Melville in her Introduction to the Paulist Press *Classics in Western Spirituality* volume dedicated to Elizabeth Seton. See Ellin Kelly and Annabelle Melville, eds., *Elizabeth Seton: Selected Writings* (New York: Paulist Press, 1987).

2. Richard Cardinal Cushing, *Blessed Mother Seton* (Boston: Daughters of St. Paul, 1963), 83.

3. Ibid., 80.

4. Ibid., 80.

5. Sister Marie Celeste, SC, ed., *Elizabeth Ann Seton: A Woman of Prayer* (Lanham, Maryland: University Press of America, 2000), 7.

6. Ibid., 15.

7. Cushing, *Blessed Mother Seton*, 61.

8. Ibid., 68.

9. Ibid., 57.

10. For a most helpful discussion of the difference between a companionship model and a patronage model in approaching the Communion of Saints, see Elizabeth Johnson, *Friends of God and Prophets: A Feminist Theological Reading of the Communion of Saints* (New York: Continuum, 1999).

11. Seton quotations from *Elizabeth Bayley Seton: Collected Writings*, vols. I & II (New City Press, 2000, 2002), eds. Regina Bechtle, SC & Judith Metz, SC; mss. ed., Ellin Kelly. Available from Vincentian Studies Institute, Chicago, IL 60614-3594.

Francis de Sales

(1567–1622)

January 24

Francis de Sales was the eldest child of a noble Savoyard family. As heir to the family fortune, Francis's father planned a legal career for him and sent him to study law. Francis, however, felt called to the priesthood and, therefore, simultaneously studied theology and Church law while earning a doctorate in civil law. In time, he obtained his father's permission to be ordained a priest. Shortly after his ordination, Francis volunteered for challenging missionary work in the Calvinist stronghold of the Chablais, on the southern shores of Lake Geneva. Warned by their Calvinist ministers not to attend his preaching, the people refused to leave their homes to hear Francis. Undaunted, Francis wrote brief tracts on the disputed articles of the faith, had them printed, and then slipped them under people's doors.

After four long years of lonely struggle, frequent reversals, and many dangers, his efforts produced the desired fruit, and the entire region returned to the Catholic faith. Francis was creative in reaching out to the people through the printed word. Owing largely to his missionary success, as well as to his growing reputation as a gifted preacher, spiritual guide, and holy man, Francis was chosen as coadjutor bishop of Geneva and ordained to that office.

While preaching Lenten sermons in Dijon, he met the future saint Jane de Chantal. In response to her desire to grow in holiness, he agreed to become her spiritual guide and directed her until his untimely death eighteen years later. In 1610, they founded the Order of the Visitation of Holy Mary, which today has monasteries throughout the world. Theirs is one of the most celebrated spiritual friendships in all of Church history. While assisting one another to the heights of sanctity, they produced one of the great spiritualities of the Church, Salesian spirituality. Francis was canonized in 1655 and declared a Doctor of the Church in 1877.

FRANCIS DE SALES

Who Was "All Things to All"

Lewis S. Fiorelli, OSFS

The collect for the January 24 feast of St. Francis de Sales reads in part: "O God, who for the salvation of souls willed that the Bishop Saint Francis de Sales become all things to all, graciously grant that, following his example, we may always display the gentleness of your charity."

These brief words from the collect capture both the essence of this most pastoral of bishops as well as the warmth of his inviting spirit. As priest and then bishop, Francis ministered to all in the gentle spirit of Jesus himself. The starting point for his own spirituality was the cultivation of a deeply personal and very loving relationship with Jesus. The goal of his tireless ministry of preaching, writing, and pastoral practice was to lead others to a similar relationship with Jesus, nourished by prayer and lived out in daily life. As Jesus lived, the Christian is to live. When Francis urges us to "be who you are and be that well," this is fundamentally his invitation to us to "live Jesus."

The biblical passage that best sums up the meaning of Jesus for Francis is: "Take my yoke upon your shoulders and learn from me, for I am gentle and humble of heart." Francis de Sales never tired of reflecting upon this passage. It was central to his personal way of living and teaching the gospel message, and it constitutes the core of his spiritual legacy to others who desire to love and live Jesus as he did.

When Jesus describes himself as humble of heart, it is an acknowledgement that the deepest core of his humanity is God's gift to him, a gift that is filled with potential and promise. As truly human and, therefore, as free before God, it was Jesus' conscious and free decision to live that gift in loving union with the Father and according to the Father's will for him. He rejoiced to be *son* and to discover in that relationship both human and spiritual fulfillment. Thus, when he says, "Learn from me," he is inviting and empowering all others to a similar humility before God; to a like embrace of the divine will; and to a similar fullness in God.

Francis de Sales embraced the example and legacy of Jesus. In his brief five and half decades among us, the gentle man from Savoy lived Jesus by a deep and abiding humility before God and a sincere, unfeigned gentleness toward every person he encountered. Like Jesus, he regarded all people as gifted by God and invited through faith to grace and glory. All his energy was directed in service of that gift in the hope of facilitating its promise and potential.

When people needed concrete, foot-washing love, his sleeves were rolled up. When they needed a comforting word, at times a challenging word, he spoke it with both clarity and charity. When the poor, the simple, and the marginalized were in need of an advocate, they found one in their bishop. For years he gave spiritual guidance to a simple hotel maid, marveling at the simplicity and strength of her faith, and learning from it. He defended a too-eager young scholar who warmed to the teachings of Galileo long before the Church did. He frequently left his lofty episcopal pulpit to play the clown for the very young children to whom he taught catechism; he learned from them as well.

These unfamiliar incidents from the life of Francis indicate just how well he learned from Jesus whom he loved. For like the Lord, he became the friend and servant of others, of *all* others. God must have looked upon Francis and discovered someone after his own heart, someone who learned so well from the gentle and humble Jesus that he could honestly say, along with St. Paul, "And the life I live now is not my own; Christ is living in me" (Gal 2:20).

We can also learn much about Francis from the three honors bestowed on him by the Church: Patron of the Catholic Press, Patron of the Deaf, and Doctor of the Love of God.

Why is Francis de Sales the Patron of the Catholic Press and, by extension, a saint for the digital world? As a newly ordained priest, Francis volunteered as a missionary to the Calvinist stronghold of the Chablais, an area just south of Geneva, Switzerland. The people there had been warned by their ministers to avoid the person and preaching of Francis. Since they were too frightened to come to him, he was determined to find a way to reach them. In that spirit, he wrote brief tracts on disputed issues of the faith, such as the place and mystery of the Church and the Petrine role of the Bishop of Rome. He had his reflections printed and slipped under the doors of people's homes. Eventually, his novel strategy paid off. After four long, arduous, and dangerous years, the entire Chablais region returned to the Catholic faith. The young missionary's creative use of the printed word in teaching the truths of the faith earned for him the title of Patron of the Press. His little tracts can now be read in an apologetical work that is variously titled as *The Catholic Controversy* or *Meditations on the Church*.

More important than what he wrote, however, is the spirit and manner in which he carried out his missionary activity. To begin with, he was determined to storm the walls of Geneva armed with charity alone, not with a show of force. His interaction with individual Calvinists was one of quiet dignity and great respect. He attempted to win them over with the pen of persuasion and simple Christian charity.

A beautiful story of a special friendship between a deaf and mute young man and his kind-hearted bishop is why St. Francis de Sales is the Patron of the Deaf. Martin worked in the bishop's residence and was totally dedicated to Francis. Because no one had been able to find a way to teach Martin about the Eucharist, he was not able to receive Holy Communion. Naturally, this caused him great sadness. The sorry plight of Martin deeply touched the tender heart of Francis. He therefore set about devising a sign language to instruct Martin on the mystery and meaning of the Eucharist. In time, Martin was able to experience the incredible joy of receiving Holy Communion from the hands of his friend. From that moment on, the bond between the two was unbreakable.

Francis was "all things to all." Many people would have perhaps counseled him to concern himself with weightier matters and more influential people. But Francis knew that Jesus would have befriended Martin and that was enough for him. This incident from the life of a busy bishop speaks powerfully to Christian leadership today!

How did Francis earn the title of Doctor of the Love of God? Most people know that Francis wrote the spiritual classic, *Introduction to the Devout Life*, in which he teaches lay women and men, in a style that is both simple and inviting, how to become holy in the midst of their busy, everyday lives. Step by step, he leads them from their simple desire for holiness to a firm resolve to take all the steps necessary to attain it. Then he teaches them how to pray, how to receive the sacraments, especially the Eucharist—"the sun of all spiritual exercises," and how to practice the "little virtues" such as gentleness, humility, charity, and kindness that are especially suitable to their many daily interactions with one another at home, in the workplace, and on the playground. He adapts everything he writes to the state and stage in life of his readers as well as to their strength and temperament.

In the *Treatise on the Love of God*, Francis teaches those same people, now devout, how to attain to the state of Christian perfection through a loving union of heart, will, and life with God's holy will for them. He does that by showing them how in concrete practice to fulfill the expectations of the first and greatest commandment: to love God above all things and in all things. He had planned to complement the *Treatise on the Love of God* with two other books, one on the love of neighbor and the other on the love of self. An early death brought on by a tireless ministry prevented the fulfillment of that hope. Still, the lofty yet practical teachings of the *Treatise on the Love of God* have rightfully earned for him the title of Doctor of the Love of God. In one place in the *Treatise* he writes: "As for ourselves…we see clearly that we can be neither truly human without having the inclination to love God more than ourselves nor truly Christian without putting this inclination into practice….This is truth. Amen" (Bk 10, ch. 10). For Francis, to be fully human and at the same time holy are but two sides of the same coin. Faith and daily life go hand in hand.

In 1610, Francis with Jane de Chantal founded the Order of the Visitation. Theirs is one of the great stories of spiritual friendship in the life of the Church. Well ahead of his time, Francis continually encouraged Jane to act in her own right and to make decisions regarding the life of the Order without first consulting him. His ideal was one of equality, mutuality, and collaboration in ministry. Francis' empowerment of Jane and many other women was centuries ahead of his time!

His determination to storm the walls of Geneva with charity alone, his simple acts of kindness toward Martin and countless others, his passionate love for God and for all of God's people, his collaborative approach to ministry, and his empowerment of women: in these and in so many other ways, Francis was truly, like Jesus, "all things to all people." Like Jesus, he interacted with everyone, from the mighty to the lowly, with both gentleness and humility, and always "as one who serves."

SALESIAN PRAYER

Father, through St. Francis de Sales,
you taught us that every act of our life,
if performed in charity and offered to you,
can be a source of great merit.
Help me,
through the intercession of St. Francis de Sales,
to consecrate every act of my life
to your greater honor and glory.
Give me the grace to live each day with Christ your son.
Help me to live each moment through love of Jesus
so that every act I perform
might become an offering to you
so that Jesus can be viewed in me every day.
May God be praised! Amen.

Paul the Apostle

(Saul of Tarsus, AD 5–67)

January 25

Paul was born in Tarsus, a city in Asia Minor, around the time of the birth of Jesus Christ. Tarsus was a city honored by Rome, and so Paul grew up with a dual identity as a Jew and a citizen of Rome. Saul was Paul's Jewish name. Long involved in his Jewish faith, Paul became a Pharisee, joining a party that was both intensely pious and deeply loyal to Judaism, studying under Gamaliel in Jerusalem. Describing himself as an early persecutor of the new Way (what came to be Christianity), Paul tried to suppress the early followers of Jesus. On his way to Damascus to arrest believers in Jesus, however, Paul experienced an appearance of the risen Christ himself, and began a twenty-year career of mission work. Although known as the "Apostle to the Gentiles," Paul certainly involved himself with Jews, urging them to become followers of Jesus, as well as breaking new ground in appealing to Gentiles to convert. He was a prominent exponent of the practice of not having Gentiles become Jews in order to follow Jesus Christ. As a founder of many Christian communities, Paul traveled widely and wrote most of the letters preserved in the New Testament. After his final arrest, he was taken to Rome where he proclaimed the Gospel from his house-prison and, according to tradition, was beheaded by the Romans around AD 67.

PAUL THE MISSIONARY

Frank DeSiano, CSP

> "To the Jews I became a Jew, in order to win Jews. To those under the law, I became as one under the law....To those outside the law I became as one outside the law....I have become all things to all people, that I might by all means save some."
>
> **(1 Cor 9:20–22)**

Paul's extraordinary missionary activity should speak powerfully in our global, multicultural universe. I believe it was his ability to span two cultures—his Jewish birth culture, and his Gentile civic culture—that made it possible for him to think consistently in terms of others. How remarkable is Paul's absorption with *the other*. We can feel his energy flowing from the pages of his writings; we can sense his footsteps, his engagement with people, and the way he presented the Good News.

This certainly had a human, personal component; after all, God uses us as we have been created. It also had a powerful moment of encounter with God. He describes his meeting of Christ (Gal 1:13ff.); that meeting is described multiple times by Luke in Acts (9:1–19; 22:3–16; 26:2–18). It was his ultimate encounter with *the other*, this God of sheer grace who unexpectedly turned Paul's life around.

Certainly, if God could engage Paul, a persecutor who tried to destroy Christ's people, did that not mean that Paul had, in turn, to engage others as well? If God makes Paul, the enemy, into an intimate friend, how could Paul avoid establishing relationships with others—whoever they might be? This fundamental insight came into a primitive Christian community that actually took quite a while to grasp its import. After all, the earliest followers of Jesus were mostly Jews from Galilee; being Jewish was part of the equation. No, says Paul. Jesus breaks through all categories, any barriers, because he is God's gift to humankind. "There is no longer Jew or Greek, there is no longer slave or free, there is no longer male and female; for all of you are one in Christ Jesus" (Gal 3:28). We should be feeling here the explosion of the fundamental categories that people used to distinguish each other. Christ has demolished these.

Paul's message of grace—God's totally free and gracious bestowal of absolute love—becomes both the message and the method of Paul. Behind all the tortured pages of theology about grace, beyond different interpretations of Paul throughout the centuries, grace basically means we are wrapped up in a field of unlimited love. Love has to expand its circle or else it is not love. Love has to be passionate, embracing, open, and persistent. It has to be "all things to all people."

Paul's own sense of universal access to his world, whether in Jerusalem or Rome, enacted his understanding of the universal access of Jesus: Christ was for all humankind, and all humankind had access to him—and to God through him. Paul could see God linking humankind together in Jesus, just as cultures had been linked in his own personal life. The experience of divine love put this linkage into motion—Paul's various journeys, his restless move from one city to another, his ongoing concern for the communities he formed.

We can think of Paul the missionary as God's chosen spreader of love. Modern people may like the word *mission*, but they are uncomfortable with the word *missionary*. Missionaries seem pushy, too self-assured, arrogant. Where does self-doubt, or multi-perspectives, or simple respect for others come in? Indeed, many modern people feel besieged by missionaries offering their formulas for everyone, even before they've engaged with people. Who wants to be a missionary?

Paul, however, missionary par excellence, can give us a very respectable way to think of mission: it's all about God's grace; God's unrestricted love, shown in the work, death, and resurrection of Jesus Christ; and given to the world through the Spirit. This is what God has done, whether people know it or not, whether people can see it or not. The missionary's task is not to berate people he or she has already judged, but to open up for people the signs of divine love already in their lives, and already working in the world.

Paul's overcoming of barriers has undoubtedly caused in history the forming of new barriers: who is a Christian and who is not; who is saved and who is not; who is a *true* Christian and who is not. We feel these fissures even in modern life. It draws some people to belief and to church; it also drives many people away from church and, sometimes too, away from belief itself. What would Paul make of all of this? How can the announcement of universal love bring universal divisions?

Paul could draw big pictures for people. In the heart of his difficult letter to the Romans, Paul treats the drama of Jews and Gentiles, straining to show that God is mysteriously bringing about the salvation of all groups. "For God has imprisoned all in disobedience, so that he may be merciful to all" (Rom 11:32). Does not this broad thinking of Paul particularly call out to us today, who see the world digitized before us through nonstop streaming Internet news? Does not Paul beg us to find patterns in it all to show the inclusive, all-encompassing love of God to a fractured and fractious human race?

Perhaps Paul feels too cranky to be conceived of as an ambassador of divine love. He certainly can get cranky—to the Galatians and to the Corinthians in particular. Even when he writes his beloved Philippians, he slips into anger mode: "Beware of the dogs, beware of the evil workers, beware of those who mutilate the flesh!" (Phil 3:2). But when you think about his crankiness, it rather parallels that of Jesus. Paul gets angry when the behavior of his communities violates the vision of divine love, just as Jesus berated those who, while claiming the mantle of teacher, rather obscured the love and mercy of his Father. We can hear Paul fuming in words similar to this: "How can you have received this gift of grace, the assurance of God's love, and then act in contradiction to it, or deny love to others?"

Paul, in one reading, pushes others to accept Jesus because he finds in Jesus the most dramatic evidence of the central core of his Gospel: Jesus shows us the unlimited love of God toward humankind. In the broken and raised body of Jesus, God has established a universal "mercy seat"—a place where God and humankind can encounter each other in reconciliation and salvation. "In Christ God was reconciling the world to himself, not counting their trespasses against them, and entrusting the message of reconciliation to us" (2 Cor 5:19).

We look at Paul from today's vantage point: a world teaming with diversity, full of great dreams and dashed hopes, replete with opportunities for coming together or falling apart. In some ways, the fundamental insight of Paul—that this is all about God's generous and unlimited love—is a message that the world has barely begun to hear. One can be passionate about this grace, and one can insist upon it for humankind, but how can anyone make it a point of division, of violence, of separation? For centuries, right up to the Second Vatican Council, Catholics and non-Catholic Christians saw the possibility of salvation for others in only begrudging ways: perhaps there was a secret desire, perhaps there was invincible ignorance.

Further reflection on certain threads in Paul's writings—"God our Savior, who desires everyone to be saved and come to the knowledge of the truth" (1 Tim 2:4)—has created a great opening for Catholics to look upon all others, whatever their religious heritage (or even lack of religious heritage). This is not about our religious brand; it's about God's sweeping love for humankind, a love that has shown itself most excellently in Jesus Christ, and a love that envelopes the world because of Christ. So this is not about

Christians versus Muslims, or Hindus, or Buddhists. This is about Christians living their faith in such a way that God's radiant love shines upon the whole world through us.

Does this, then, make Christianity relative or unnecessary? As St. Paul might say: hardly! It brings into clarity the very importance of Christian faith, and the very reason to invite people to experience it. The invitation is to spread love, to experience it unreservedly and to live it fully, one of the greatest missions one can imagine. God's love, total and pure (unlike most human love), is needed so drastically by our world. For God's love calls us into being, glistens in our minds through wisdom, gnaws at our hearts in conscience, pushes us beyond the boundaries of our measly and selfish relationships, and remains the standard according to which we are, and will be, judged. To know and respond to this love, purifying and saving, remains the central decision of any woman or man.

To people today, being missionary can look sectarian. That is why Paul is so essential for our contemporary world. We can look past the fanatic we have made Paul into, and see the expansive missionary vision that was compelled to declare God's love to everyone, and to insist on a grace beyond laws, beyond boundaries, beyond tags, beyond language, and beyond pettiness. He found all this in Jesus. He invited others to find this in Jesus. And he urges us to articulate a message to the world: come; find total love, true love, in the God of Jesus.

This lays a double spiritual burden upon all believers, particularly those who follow in the path of Paul. First, do we not have to experience what Paul did? Do we not have to be swept up and away by this empowering love? Do we not have to let this love sear our eyes until they view the world as saturated by divine love? Do we not have to let this love break open the stony edges of our hearts until we love as God loves? Can there be an examination of conscience keener than this?

Second, we have to reflect on Paul's edginess and restlessness. We have to rethink what made Paul hit those dusty roads and cross unfriendly seas. Sure, he had an urgent vision. Sure, he thought the world would end a little sooner than we surmise. But was he not driven most of all by an experience of God that he thought was crucial for the world? Behind it all, is this not a perfectly apt, and urgent, message for today, for us, and for our world?

Love can do funny things to us. It can make us jealous, or nervous, or persistent, or petulant. The purer our experience of love, the more love purifies our motives, making us generous, and kind, and other-focused, and eager for the good of others, as Paul tells us in his famous hymn about love (1 Cor 13). So in the end, with all that love can make us, it can also make us missionaries, bearers of divine love to the world, as generously and graciously as God has done this in Jesus, not resting until "God may be all in all" (1 Cor 15:28), that is, until "absolute love may be all in all."

PAUL'S PRAYER FROM EPHESIANS 3:14–19

For this reason I kneel before the Father,
from whom every family in heaven and on earth is named,
that he may grant you in accord with the riches of his glory to be
strengthened with power through his Spirit in the inner self,
and that Christ may dwell in your hearts through faith; that you,
rooted and grounded in love,
may have strength to comprehend with all the holy ones what is
the breadth and length and height and depth,
and to know the love of Christ that surpasses knowledge, so that
you may be filled with all the fullness of God. (RNAB)

Martin Luther King, Jr.

(1929–1968)

Third Monday of January

Martin Luther King, Jr., was born on January 15, 1929, in Atlanta, Georgia, and was ordained a Baptist minister at age 18. He graduated from Morehouse College and Crozer Theological Seminary. In 1955, he earned a doctoral degree in systematic theology from Boston University. In Boston he met and later married Coretta Scott, and they had two sons and two daughters.

Dr. King accepted his first pastorate at the Dexter Avenue Baptist Church in Montgomery, Alabama. While he was serving as pastor, Rosa Parks was arrested for refusing to give up her seat on a bus to a white man. As a response, King promoted the Montgomery Bus boycott, which became a turning point in the civil rights struggle, attracting national attention. The boycott lasted for several months, and the Supreme Court eventually ruled that racial segregation on public transportation was illegal. King soon became a national figure.

In 1957, King helped found the Southern Christian Leadership Conference (SCLC), an organization of black churches and ministers that aimed to challenge racial segregation. The SCLC goal was to provide leadership and organization in the fight for civil rights. The leadership encouraged the use of nonviolent marches, demonstrations, and peaceful protests, based on the writings of Thoreau and the actions of Mohandas Gandhi. King's challenges to segregation and racial discrimination helped convince many white Americans to support the cause of civil rights in the United States.

Dr. King played a major part in many nonviolent protests in the fight for desegregation and equal rights. He was arrested numerous times. In 1963, numerous "sit-ins" were staged in Birmingham, Alabama, to protest segregation in restaurants. King was arrested during one of these. While imprisoned, he wrote his famous *Letter from Birmingham Jail*, arguing that only through visible protests would progress be made. He insisted that it was an individual's duty to protest and in fact, disobey unjust laws.

On August 28, 1963, the March on Washington took place, the largest demonstration of its kind up to then. While speaking from the Lincoln Memorial, King delivered his famous "I Have a Dream" speech to more than 250,000 civil rights supporters. He was an inspirational speaker with the capacity to move and uplift his audiences, offering a vision of hope, while capturing the injustice of the time.

The speech and the march created the political momentum that resulted in the Civil Rights Act of 1964, prohibiting segregation in public accommodations and discrimination in education and employment. Dr. King was named *Time* Magazine's Man of the Year and awarded the 1964 Nobel Prize for peace at the age of thirty-five.

On March 7, 1965, a group of protestors attempted a march from Selma to Montgomery, Alabama. King was not part of this march because he had wanted to delay its start date. However, the march was extremely significant because it was met by terrible police brutality, captured on film. These images made a huge impact on those not directly involved, and as a result, there was a public outcry for change. The march was attempted again and the protestors successfully arrived in Montgomery on March 25, 1965, where they heard King speak at the Capitol.

Throughout 1966 and 1967, King increasingly turned his focus to the redistribution of the nation's economic wealth to overcome entrenched black poverty. In the spring of 1968, he went to Memphis, Tennessee, to support striking black garbage workers. While speaking from a balcony at the Lorraine Motel in Memphis, he was assassinated. While James Earl Ray was arrested and charged, there have been and still are questions about his guilt and whether there was a larger conspiracy at work.

Dr. Martin Luther King, Jr., Day is celebrated the third Monday of January.

DR. MARTIN LUTHER KING, JR.

Preacher of the Gospel

D. Bruce Nieli, CSP

Martin Luther King, Jr., as a master of rhetoric and master of the Gospel, had the remarkable ability to profoundly inspire the world. Through his preaching and witness, the culture of an entire nation was transformed and converted. Some suggest the election of the first African American President of the United States flowed directly from the evangelistic impact of Martin Luther King. The culture of a people was cultivated by a great precursor and prophet, so that rich fruit could be harvested decades later. King always wanted first and foremost to be known as a preacher of the Gospel, the spark that got the fire of the civil rights movement going.

As a prophet, Martin Luther King undoubtedly felt himself at times to be "a voice crying in the wilderness"—witness his *Letter from Birmingham Jail*, challenging his fellow clergy to fight for justice and equality. To be sure, this loneliness and isolation was especially heightened when he took the courageous stand of protesting the war in Vietnam. As the youngest person up until that time to win the Nobel Peace Prize, King had much in common with Jeremiah, called from the womb to "pluck up and to pull down."[1] Yet Martin Luther King was very much a *reconciler*. After all, his great dream was to have "the sons of former slaves and the sons of former slave owners" to sit down, hand in hand, "at the table of brotherhood." He sought to reconcile America to its fundamental principle of liberty and justice for all. In the spirit of Paulist founder and Servant of God Isaac Thomas Hecker, he desired our nation to live out unity amidst diversity, or, in terms of our country's founding motto, to be in fact *e pluribus unum* (out of many, one!). By God's grace, we have, as Catholics, the ideal table of brotherhood and sisterhood, the table of the Eucharist. King's vision of an America united at a table open to all religions, classes, races, and demographic groups reconciles nicely with the welcoming table of the liturgy.

Dr. King was clearly a committed ecumenist and interreligious advocate. Rarely has a movement in United States history experienced such active and united participation from so many different faiths as the movement that he led so effectively, the struggle for civil rights. Protestant ministers marched with Catholic nuns and priests as well as Jewish rabbis and leaders and representatives of the myriad American religious denominations, to ensure that religious liberty was guaranteed but also proactive. King's niece, Alveda King, is similarly active ecumenically and interreligiously as an influential leader in the contemporary pro-life movement. Her uncle would undoubtedly have shouted a resounding *amen* to Pope John Paul II's statement in his encyclical *Redemptoris Missio*[2] that the Holy Spirit is "mysteriously present in every human heart." His heroic witness of nonviolent resistance to bigoted and cruel aggression puts him very much in sync with that of Buddhist monks and nuns in present-day Tibet.

Martin Luther King would display a connection to the Holy Spirit in other ways as well. The "I have a dream" section of his famous speech was actually a departure from the prepared text. He most assuredly opened his heart at a crucial point in his delivery to the same Spirit present in the hearts of the multitude of the hearers he gazed upon at the Washington Mall, to come up with arguably the most famous oratorical presentation of the twentieth century. Here we also see a connection with Father Isaac Hecker, whose belief in personal response to the Holy Spirit was the foundation of his spirituality.

America and the world, so riddled with violence, are sorely in need of spiritual witnesses of the caliber of Martin Luther King and Mohandas Gandhi. Will swords ever be beaten into plowshares and spears into pruning hooks (Isa 2:4)? The violence contributing to a culture of death can ultimately be conquered by the nonviolence of a culture of life. King so beautifully embodied the peace of the Prince of Peace, who counseled us not to take up the sword lest we perish by the sword (Matt 26:52). And like his Lord and Savior, Jesus Christ, Martin would as a young man perish by the sword.

PRAYER OF MARTIN LUTHER KING, JR.[3]

O God, we thank you for the fact that you have inspired
men and women in all nations and in all cultures.
We call you different names: some call you Allah;
some call you Elohim; some call you Jehovah;
some call you Brahma; some call you the Unmoved Mover.
But we know that these are all names for one and the same God.
Grant that we will follow you and become so committed to
your way and your kingdom
that we will be able to establish in our lives
and in this world a brother and sisterhood, that we will be able
to establish here a kingdom of understanding,
where men and women will live together as brothers and sisters
and respect the dignity and worth of every human being.
In the name and spirit of Jesus. Amen.

NOTES

1. Jeremiah 1:10.

2. *Redemptoris Missio* (The Mission of the Redeemer), 29

3. Martin Luther King Jr., *Thou, Dear God: Prayers that Open Hearts and Spirits*, edited by Lewis V. Baldwin (Boston: Beacon Press, 2012), 45.

Thomas Aquinas

(1225–1274)

January 28

St. Thomas Aquinas was born in 1225, the son of Landulph, Count of Aquino. At the age of seventeen, Thomas joined the Dominican friars in Naples. Some family members opposed his plan and tried to break his resolve, but their efforts were unsuccessful. Thomas persevered in his vocation, made his profession in Naples, and studied in Cologne with St. Albert the Great. He was given the nickname "dumb ox" because of his quiet manner and hulking size. However, he excelled as a student. At the age of twenty-two, he taught in Cologne and published his first works. After four years he was sent to Paris to study for his doctorate.

At Paris, he was honored with the friendship of the king, St. Louis, with whom he frequently dined. In 1261, Pope Urban IV called him to Rome to teach. Thomas was a prolific writer; his writings filled twenty large tomes, characterized by brilliant thought and lucid expression. As the foremost classical proponent of natural theology, he greatly influenced Western thought. Much of modern philosophy was conceived in development or refutation of his ideas, particularly in the areas of ethics, natural law, metaphysics, and political theory. He is best known for his works *Summa Theologica* and *Summa contra Gentiles*. While en route to the second Council of Lyons, he became sick and died at the Cistercian monastery of Fossa Nuova in 1274.

Thomas Aquinas is one of the most influential philosophers and theologians of all time in the tradition of Scholasticism. He was canonized in 1323 and declared Doctor of the Church by Pope Pius V. He is also known as *Doctor Angelicus*, *Doctor Communis*, and *Doctor Universalis* and is the patron of universities and students.

THOMAS AQUINAS

The Angelic Doctor

Dominic F. Doyle

St. Thomas Aquinas was born into a family of minor nobility around 1225 in Roccasecca, halfway between Rome and Naples. Spurning his family's wishes, he joined the new mendicant Order of Preachers and, after a highly productive career teaching and writing, died in 1274. Unlike the charismatic St. Francis of Assisi, Thomas for the most part lived an uneventful life of theological inquiry and religious education. One must, therefore, look not to biographical drama but to intellectual insight to appreciate his spirituality.

As one of the great medieval theologians, Aquinas towers over the intellectual landscape of Catholicism. His work was once distorted into an aggressive, rationalistic defense against modernity—what Hans Urs von Balthasar chastised as a hyper-organized, grumpy Thomism—and it briefly fell out of favor in the wake of Vatican II's return to biblical and patristic sources and its *rapprochement* with modern ideas. Now it enjoys a remarkable and ecumenical renaissance. Catholic theologians are discovering the rich biblical grounding and deep spiritual vision of his work, while Protestant thinkers are coming to appreciate the theological value of his profound metaphysical insight.

The most basic metaphysical insight for Thomas, the deep wellspring of his spirituality, concerns the very *nature* of divinity.

"What is God?" he used to ask his childhood tutors. By the time he became a teacher, Thomas turned the question around and began by asking what God is not. For Aquinas, God is not another item of furniture in the universe alongside other items, only bigger, better, and stronger. In his metaphysical language, God is not one more effect alongside other effects that are caused by something else. For while all finite things are caused by another, God cannot receive existence from another, else there would be something "behind" God giving life to God, and so God would not be God, but something caused. So it follows that to be God is to be the uncaused cause of all. What this means, we do not know. But we can at least be precise about our ignorance: God's essence—what God is—must be identical with God's existence. And since causes produce effects according to their essence, and since God's essence is God's existence, then God's proper effect must be existence. In a nutshell, God is the infinite, unrestricted act of existence, existing in and through Himself, not caused by another, but rather the ultimate cause of everything that is. Put simply, God is the Source of all that exists, the reason why there is something, not nothing, the unexplainable explanation for why there is a universe at all.

What does all this have to with spirituality? Consider the following two conclusions drawn from the same premise established above. As infinite Creator, God utterly transcends the world, because what is infinite and uncaused cannot be contained in, or grasped by, what is finite and caused. But from this same premise—God's infinity—we can draw the seemingly opposite conclusion: God is deeply present in the world, for what is infinite has no end and so must be everywhere. There is nowhere where God is not. Indeed, since existence is the most basic principle of any thing, God, as the source of existence, is intimately present to everything. Here we see the metaphysical basis for St. Ignatius of Loyola's conviction that God can be found in all things. All of creation is to be approached positively, as the place where we encounter God. Conversely, to disparage creation is to disparage the Creator. And we should add for our own context that to despoil creation is to sin against God. Aquinas' medieval metaphysics, far from being irrelevant today, in fact provides the grounds for an urgently needed ecological spirituality, which seeks to protect creation from exploitation by fostering a deep sense of the sacredness of all creation as participating in divine life.

From this metaphysical insight into the nature of divinity flows a key realization for any life-giving spirituality: God and creation are not competing causes. More of one does not mean less of the other. Being engaged with God and caring about this world is not like trying to support the Red Sox and the Yankees at the same time. Rather, it is more like supporting a baseball team while also loving baseball. The two cannot be separated. In the very act of loving baseball, you will root for one team; and in the very act of supporting a team, you thereby display your love for baseball. Returning to theology, we can say that God and creation stand in a relation of direct, not inverse, proportion. An active engagement with one brings the person into closer contact with the other. Seek God, and you must approach Him through His effects—everything that is, the world around you. But immerse yourself in creation, and you will soon find that it points beyond itself to a transcendent cause.

To believe in a Creator God, then, is to be poised between joy at the wonder of existence and gratitude for the Giver who bestowed it. It is to delight in the goodness that flows through creation, while looking upstream to the Source. It is to seek God in all things, but in the knowledge that "where God is, is not God."[1] This spirituality of creation allows us to embrace the goods of the world without leaving our claw marks in them as they, or indeed we, slip away. For to be created is to be finite, and so to be finite is no bad thing. The inevitable limits of creaturely finitude are not, at least in principle, reason for permanent lament. To the contrary, they are the channels through which created things can bring forth some particular aspect of God's infinite perfection. Aquinas's creation metaphysics, then, forms the basis of a profound spirituality that at once engages the world and honors God. In fact, it insists that one honors God precisely through engaging the world, but without thereby making an idol of anything in the world.

As a specifically Christian thinker, Aquinas could assert without hesitation that as God is the source of existence, so Christ is the source of grace. What is grace? In the phrase of a modern Thomist, Karl Rahner, grace is the point at which God is no longer distant, silent horizon, but rather intimate, forgiving presence. It is the process by which the natural longing for God is healed and perfected. For while it is true that the human person, created in the image of God, has a natural desire for its divine exemplar, it nonetheless needs God's help to overcome the limits not only of finitude but also of sin. The *humanum* must, therefore, be recreated by grace. In the words of one contemporary commentator, if creation brings life from nothing, then grace brings new life from the deeper nothingness of death and sin.[2] Ordinary human desires to know and to love are thus enveloped by the extraordinary—because unexpected and unmerited—gift of God's Spirit that floods the heart (Rom 5:5).

Based on Christ, this grace gives specific form to the spiritual quest. It patterns the person to the shape of Christ's self-giving love that follows the will of the Father, come what may. This love does not deplete the self but rather brings it into contact with the deepest source of goodness and new life as it faces seemingly intractable conflict and hopelessness. The spirituality advanced by Aquinas, then, is not a vague feeling based on general metaphysical claims and divorced from the messiness of history. Nor does it oppose religion. To the contrary, it is based on the central doctrine of the Christian religion, the doctrine of the Trinity, and is the living principle of the Church. Grounded on the saving life, death, and resurrection of Jesus Christ, as made real for us here and now by the gift of the Holy Spirit, it brings the person into the enveloping love of the Father. A general spirituality inspired by creation metaphysics thus undergoes a journey of intensification as it becomes a paschal dramatics, a Christian spirituality.

PANGE LINGUA

Sing, my tongue, the Saviour's glory,
of His Flesh, the mystery sing;
of the Blood, all price exceeding,
shed by our Immortal King,
destined, for the world's redemption,
from a noble Womb to spring.

Of a pure and spotless Virgin
born for us on earth below,
He, as Man, with man conversing,
stayed, the seeds of truth to sow;
then He closed in solemn order
wondrously His Life of woe.

On the night of that Last Supper,
seated with His chosen band,
He, the Paschal Victim eating,
first fulfils the Law's command;
then as Food to His Apostles
gives Himself with His own Hand.

Word-made-Flesh, the bread of nature
by His Word to Flesh He turns;
wine into His Blood He changes;
what though sense no change discerns?
Only be the heart in earnest,
faith her lesson quickly learns.

Down in adoration falling,
This great Sacrament we hail,
O'er ancient forms of worship
Newer rites of grace prevail;
Faith will tell us Christ is present,
When our human senses fail.

To the Everlasting Father,
And the Son who made us free
And the Spirit, God proceeding
From them Each eternally,
Be salvation, honour, blessing,
Might and endless majesty.
Amen. Alleluia.[3]

NOTES

1. I owe this phrase to Nicholas Lash.

2. I am indebted to Robert Sokolowski's reflections in *Christian Faith and Human Understanding* (Washington, DC: Catholic University of America Press, 2006), 70.

3. English translation by Edward Caswall.

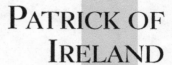

Patrick of Ireland

(389–492)

March 17

Patrick was born in Britain in AD 389. Pirates captured him at age sixteen and sold him into slavery in Ireland. During his captivity, he turned to God in prayer. Later, he went to Rome to become a priest and was ordained by Saint Germanus. Eventually as a bishop, he was sent to preach the Gospel in Ireland. Although there was a small number of Christians on the island when Patrick arrived, most Irish practiced a nature-based pagan religion, centered around a rich tradition of oral legend and myth. Patrick learned this culture and incorporated the rituals into his preaching on Christianity. For instance, he used bonfires at Easter since the Irish were used to honoring their gods with fire. He also superimposed a sun, a powerful Irish symbol, onto the Christian cross to create what is now called the Celtic cross. Over forty years, he converted many local people and worked miracles in the name of Jesus.

PATRICK

Missionary to the Irish

John E. Collins, CSP

Holding a shamrock, Saint Patrick explained the Trinity to the Irish people. In that simple action, Patrick revealed his genius. Already an established religious symbol among the Irish, the shamrock was an important plant to Druids who believed it had medical properties and mystical powers. The shamrock's association with the number three, a sacred number in ancient numerology, assured the Druids it could ward off evil spirits. So when Patrick held up the shamrock it already carried its own story and meaning. Patrick tweaked the meaning and gave it a new narrative. No longer just a Druidical symbol, Patrick transformed the shamrock into a Christian icon.[1]

Patrick's genius was to tell the story of Christianity from *within* the story of the Irish rather than impose the Christian story *on* the Irish. This was the key to Patrick's success. The failure of so many prior missionaries to tell the story effectively to native people came about because they didn't bother to understand the people they were trying to evangelize. They took the culture and imposed it on their listeners, often with disdain and condescension. No wonder the ancient Irish could never quite connect the Christian faith to their own culture! Indeed, the power of Jesus and his story never took serious root among them until Patrick's arrival.

Patrick's methods were very much akin to those of Servant of God Isaac Hecker, who started the Paulist Fathers in 1858 as the first religious order of priests founded in the United States. Hecker's genius was to tell Christianity's story *within* the American story rather than imposing it from without. Hecker believed the American story was fruitful soil for the Christian story. Each would complement the other—America enhanced by the Gospel of Jesus, the Gospel in turn enhanced by the American story. Taking our national motto, *E pluribus unum*—literally "out of many, one"—Hecker demonstrated that more than any other religious vehicle, the Catholic Church could bring about such a unity so that "all may be one." The "many" could be one in the community of the Catholic Church. Thus, "unity" would offer the ideal complement to America's pride in individual liberty, self-reliance, and independence.

For his part, Saint Patrick so effectively infused Christianity within Irish sensibilities that the Irish made Patrick's shamrock a symbol of Irish identity and unity. It ultimately became the primary sign of Irish independence, spiritually sustaining the rebellions of 1798, finding its place within a popular street ballad, "The Wearing of the Green": "They were hanging men and women for the wearing of the green" (shamrock). The Irish continued to promulgate the shamrock and the song throughout the reign of Queen Victoria (1819–1901) and beyond. Thus, while maintaining its spiritual roots, the shamrock also became a symbol of national pride.

J. B. Bury's well-respected Patrick biography, *Ireland's Saint*,[2] remains the authoritative reference to this day. From Bury we glean the following: Patrick was born around AD 389 in Britain; his father, Calpurnius, was an ordained Catholic deacon, and his grandfather an ordained Catholic priest. They educated Patrick in the Christian faith and taught him the Christian scriptures. At the age of sixteen, he was taken captive and brought to Ireland as a slave. There he worked for six years before escaping by ship to Gaul, where he began his journey back to his family. Along the continental coast, Patrick visited a number of great monasteries, spiritual havens he may have heard about from travelers through Ireland during his captivity. These visits fascinated him and filled him with wonder, and added years to his return voyage to Britain.

Bury writes: "Patrick found a refuge in the island cloister of Honoratus...how easily he could have been moved by the ascetic attractions of the monastery to interrupt his homeward journey and lead a religious life in the *sacrae solitudines* of Lerinus for a few years. The years Patrick spent at Lerinus exercised an abiding influence on him. Monastic societies became a principal and indispensible element in his idea of a Christian church."[3]

Patrick recounts he had a vision, a few years after returning home. "I saw a man coming, as it were from Ireland. His name was Victoricus, and he carried many letters, and he gave me one of them. I read the heading: 'The Voice of the Irish.' As I began the letter, I imagined in that moment that I heard the voice of those very people who were near the woods of Foclut, which is beside the western sea—and they cried out, as with one voice: 'We appeal to you, holy servant boy, to come and walk among us.'"[4]

Christianity had already been introduced to Ireland even before Patrick's arrival. It came through commerce with Ireland from Spain and Gaul and Briton. Patrick, however, did organize the Church and gave it a uniquely Irish tone as distinct from a purely Roman one. The church in Ireland became famously native following Patrick's respect for the culture. As noted, his *modus operandi* was akin to that of Isaac Hecker who worked within the American culture to explain Catholicism to a skeptical American audience. Furthermore, Patrick loved Irish culture and the Irish people. Patrick wanted to enrich both the people and culture of Ireland by bringing the true faith, a faith that would not destroy, but rather uphold Irish culture.

In his *Confessions*, Patrick couches his self-reflection in suprisingly self-deprecating language that would have little appeal today. Patrick writes, "I have been exalted beyond measure by the Lord, and I was not worthy that he should grant me this while I know most certainly that poverty and failure suit me better than wealth and delight."[5] Patrick, however, affirms over and over his trust in the Lord: "Cast your burdens on the Lord, he will sustain you."

The Lord was indeed his salvation, his strength; not his own worthiness, but the Lord's power sustained him. During a long, forty-day fast high on a mountain that became known as Croagh Patrick near Westport in county Mayo, Patrick identified a sacred site that had existed before Christianity's arrival, where snakes attacked him. The legend goes that he retaliated by driving them all into the sea. Snakes were associated with the Druids, who had large tattoos of snakes on their arms. Driving the snakes out reduced the claim the Druids had over the Irish people. Thus Christianity could move into the power vacuum that was left.[6]

Patrick did not have an easy time of it. He writes in his *Confessions*, "from time to time I gave rewards to the Kings as well as making payments to their sons who travel with me; not withstanding which, they seized me with my companions, and that day most avidly desired to kill me. But my time had not yet come. They plundered everything they found on us anyway, and fettered me in irons; and on the fourteenth day the Lord freed me from their power, and whatever they had of ours was given back to us for the sake of God on account of the indispensible friends whom we had made."[7]

Patrick never lost heart, though, and even boasts of the thousands he baptized, the clergy he ordained, and the confirmations he administered. Isaac Hecker also encountered many difficulties in founding the Missionary Society of St. Paul, the Paulist Fathers. En route to Rome in the 1850s to plead his case for a new approach to mission in America, he was dismissed from the Redemptorists, the religious community he entered after his conversion to the Catholic Church. In addition, he encountered many delays in Rome before he could plead his case to Holy Father Pius IX. Discouraged as he may have been in his quest to form a new religious order of priests in America, Hecker, like Patrick, relied on the Holy Spirit's strength to sustain him and be his strength. I believe Father Hecker selected Saint Patrick as a patron saint of the Paulist Fathers because he saw in Patrick echoes of his own approach to mission and desired to hold him up as a model in mission for all Paulists to emulate. Both men saw that the way to invite people to hear the story of Jesus was to tell it in their language, in their culture, and in familiar idioms. Patrick ever remains a model for all missionaries: Get into the story of the people you are trying to evangelize and speak from there.

ST. PATRICK'S BREASTPLATE

Christ with me, Christ before me
Christ behind me, Christ in me
Christ beneath me, Christ above me
Christ on my right, Christ on my left
Christ when I lie down
Christ when I arise
Christ in the heart of everyone who speaks of me
Christ in every eye that sees me
Christ in every ear that hears me. Amen

NOTES

1. http://www.wisegeek.com/who-is-saint-patrick.htm.
2. J. B. Bury, *Ireland's Saint*, 1905 with annotations Jon M. Sweeney (Brewster, MA: Paraclete Press, 2008), 63.
3. Ibid.
4. *The Confessions of Saint Patrick* (circa 380–460 CE): http://www.ccel.org/ccel/patrick/confession.html.
5. *Confessions* #55.
6. http://www.wisegeek.com/who-is-saint-patrick.htm.
7. *Confessions* #52.

JOSEPH

Husband of Mary

March 19

Saint Joseph, the foster father of Jesus Christ, was the husband of Mary and believed to be the descendant of King David. Joseph was a skilled carpenter, a man of tremendous faith. When an angel came to him in a dream with the truth about Mary's baby, he did not question it, but rather wed her. He loved and cared for Jesus as his son. He fled to Egypt with his family to protect them and then settled in Nazareth. It is believed that Joseph died before Jesus began his public ministry.

He is the patron of workers and fathers. His feast day is March 19. Already a patron saint of Mexico, Canada, and Belgium, in 1870, Joseph was declared the patron of the universal church by Pope Pius IX. In 1955, Pope Pius XII established May 1 as the "Feast of St. Joseph the Worker" to counter the Communists' May Day.

JOSEPH

Model of Eloquent Silence

Thomas Stegman, SJ

All of us know, or have known, someone who can be characterized as "a man of few words." Typically, such a person is highly regarded because he has a sense of gravitas. On those occasions when he does speak, our ears perk up because we recognize that what he has to say is thoughtful and wise—and expressed in an economy of words.

Does St. Joseph fit this picture? My sense is yes, based on the biblical testimony about him. To be sure, that testimony is sparse. The infancy narratives in the Gospels of Matthew and Luke provide most of the material from which we can glean a sketch of Joseph, especially Matthew's account. A close reading of these texts, however, leads to a remarkable discovery: Joseph is never portrayed as speaking. He is not only "a man of few words"; he is "a man of no words"! What we hear from Joseph is…silence. Yet, what an eloquent silence it is, for silence underlies and catalyzes all the admirable features of his character that are relevant for Christian life and spirituality today.

Joseph's distinguishing attribute, according to Matthew, is that he was "a just man" (1:19). The adjective here is *dikaios*, which can also be rendered "righteous." At root, the term expresses an unflinching commitment to enact God's will. From a Jewish (and thus Joseph's) perspective, to be *dikaios* is intimately linked with covenant faithfulness, with living in right relationship with

God and with others. It, therefore, entails fidelity to Torah, to what God has revealed in Scripture. As such, it requires silence for studying and listening to sacred texts.

Matthew provides a hint of Joseph's reflective posture regarding the Torah when the latter learned of Mary's pregnancy. The verb *enthymeomai* (1:20) denotes "ponder" or "reflect in one's heart." Joseph's initial decision to quietly divorce Mary, rather than publicly shame her, manifests such prayerful pondering of God's revealed word. The sense of magnanimous compassion towards Mary that accompanied his commitment to the Law is striking. Might Jesus' way of embodying the Torah—"Take my yoke upon you, and learn from me; for I am gentle and humble in heart" (Matt 11:29)—have been learned, at least in part, from his foster father's example of obedience to God, an example rooted in prayerful silence? I suggest so.

We know, of course, that Joseph did not divorce Mary. That is because he listened to God's will manifested to him in a way other than his study and knowledge of Torah. Like his namesake, the firstborn of Jacob and Rachel's two sons (cf. Gen 37—50), Joseph paid attention to his dreams in the silence of sleep. Matthew's version of the Annunciation story relates how the angel Gabriel communicated to Joseph via a dream. There he learned about the initiative of God to reach out to us in love, about the divine source of Jesus' conception, and about the mission of Jesus to "save his people from their sins"(1:21).

Joseph's commitment to enacting God's will was generous and immediate. In taking pregnant Mary as his wife, he exemplifies openness to a new way of listening, as well as the courage to act on what was revealed to him. Joseph models alertness to the surprising ways in which God's Spirit leads and acts (cf. John 3:8), an alertness—grounded in silence—that can also shed new light on understanding Scripture. In fact, in the course of narrating Joseph's dream, Matthew explains how Mary's conception of Jesus fulfilled the prophecy concerning Emmanuel, "God with us" (Isa 7:14; Matt 1:23).

The Annunciation revelation was not the only dream Joseph received in the silence of slumber. He also learned about Herod's murderous intentions against the infant Jesus and was instructed to take Mary and the child to safe haven in Egypt (Matt 2:13). Some years later, he discovered in a dream when it was safe to return with them to Israel (2:19–20), although he was now directed to settle in the district of Galilee rather than Judah (2:22). Joseph's attentiveness to God's promptings had unexpected, difficult, yet ultimately life-giving consequences.

While Matthew's infancy narrative draws on the motif of divine revelations bestowed in sleep-induced dreams, I propose that Joseph's dreams be read on a metaphorical level as well. Thus, one can also say he exemplifies what it means "to dream big." Or, to put things in another way, he is a model of the prayerful silence necessary for eliciting, and getting in touch with, those deep-down desires that form part of the stuff of discernment. Careful attention to the Spirit's promptings can lead us, like Joseph, to leave behind the familiar, go to new and foreign "lands," and establish a new "home" in places we never would have considered had we stayed within our accustomed paradigms.

Joseph's silence is also integral to the two dimensions of his vocation celebrated by the Church's liturgy. March 19 is the Solemnity of St. Joseph, Husband of Mary. Joseph's loving, protective care of Mary and Jesus is certainly intimated in the dramatic stories of the family's flight to Egypt and subsequent return to Israel upon the death of Herod (Matt 2:13–23). We also get a glimpse of Joseph's (and Mary's) religious devotion in Luke's accounts of the circumcision and naming of Jesus (Luke 2:21), the purification and presentation in the Temple (2:22–40), and the Passover pilgrimage to Jerusalem when Jesus was age twelve (2:41–52). The figure of Joseph remains largely in the background of these stories. Generous and selfless love for Mary and Jesus, humble and protective care for them, and commitment to faith and piety—this portrait offers wholesome content and meaning to "the strong, silent type," the type Joseph so nobly embodied.

The second liturgical celebration is May 1, the (optional) Memorial of St. Joseph the Worker. According to Matthew 13:55, Joseph was a *tektōn*, a "carpenter." While this notice has led to his depiction as a poor laborer, it may very well indicate that Joseph was a skilled artisan. As a carpenter, he worked long hours in voiceless silence, the silence necessary for creativity and professional precision. It was in Joseph's workshop that Jesus learned carpentry (cf. Mark 6:3) as well as the dignity of labor. According to (albeit later) Talmudic tradition, carpenters were renowned for being wise. Joseph's quiet workshop may very well have been, in effect, a "school" for the one who astonished so many people by his wisdom.

For a man from whom no words have been recorded for posterity (at least in the New Testament), Joseph has a lot to say. His silence speaks eloquently, for it was the source and characteristic of his exemplary qualities—prayerful reflection on and fidelity to Torah/Scripture; commitment to God's will; alertness and openness to God's surprising ways; loving, protective care of Mary and Jesus; creative and dignified labor. May St. Joseph intercede for us so that we may imitate his eloquent silence.

PRAYER TO ST. JOSEPH, PATRON OF WORKERS[1]

St. Joseph, Patron of Workers,
Help us to respect the dignity of all workers.
Help us to learn about and to care about
Workers who do not have fair wages,
  just benefits, safe working environments.
Help us to raise our voices for justice for workers.
Help us to ask our government and our representatives
To develop policies that create jobs with dignity.

You taught your son
The value of work and the joy of work well done.

Teach us these lessons.
Guide us in our own work
And in the work of justice
We are all called to participate in.
Renew our strength and commitment
Each day as we face the work ahead
As we labor for the common good of all.
Amen.

NOTES

1. Prayer by Education for Justice, a project of the Center of Concern.

Archbishop Oscar Romero

(1917–1980)

March 24

Oscar Arnulfo Romero y Galdámez was born in Ciudad Barrios in 1917 in the eastern part of El Salvador. He was ordained in Rome in 1942 and assigned to the Diocese of San Miguel in 1944. The people enjoyed his sermons, which were broadcast on the radio. Over the next thirty years, Romero worked in El Salvador, and in February 1977, he became archbishop of San Salvador. Soon afterwards, soldiers attacked protesters in the capital, and Romero began to see that the people in power were violent men. The few but wealthy families that ran the country supported this violent regime.

In response to popular resistance to the injustices, death squads committed murders in the cities, while soldiers killed as they wished in the countryside. During this time, poor people suffered the most. As Archbishop Romero spoke out against violence, crowds of people came to listen in person, and others crowded around their radios to hear him. His message was that Jesus was suffering in them. His message to the murderers was that they were crucifying Jesus when they killed others.

Romero knew his life was in danger. In an interview weeks before his death, he said that his blood would be the seed for liberty for his people. On March 24, 1980, the archbishop was shot dead while celebrating the eucharist in the chapel of Divine Providence where he lived and worked. His death was like a seed that grew steadily in the hearts of the poor people in El Salvador. He said, "And if they kill me, I will rise again in the Salvadoran people." Today the memory of Oscar Romero is treasured by the people of El Salvador and by countless Christians across the world. Romero stands as an example of faith and trust in Jesus.

His story inspires many people to share Jesus' love by caring for hurting people. On the tenth anniversary of his death, his successor appointed a postulator for the cause of his canonization. After investigations into Romero's life, work, and writings, the archdiocese submitted the results to the Vatican's Congregation for the Causes of Saints in 1997. To date, Rome has not taken the matter any further, probably due to the institutional Church's continued mistrust of liberation theology, but Romero's cause may now go forward with the new pope, Francis. In July 1998, the Church of England unveiled a statue of Romero on the west door of Westminster Abbey in London, as part of a monument to the memory of ten twentieth-century martyrs, and set aside March 24 in their liturgical calendar for the commemoration of Oscar Romero.

OSCAR ROMERO

Model of Conversion

O. Ernesto Valiente

Three decades after his martyrdom in 1980, Romero remains a challenging, even unsettling saint. To be sure, the memory of his practical and transforming love is a source of comfort and hope. But his witness interrogates and challenges us to carry on in his fashion. In this, Romero is a saintly man, who exemplifies the charism of conversion. His own spiritual transformation, at the age of sixty, sheds light on his ministry and on what he envisioned for the Salvadoran people. It also illuminates what Christ envisions for his Church today.

On February 23, 1977, after two years as bishop of Santiago de Maria—a small diocese east of the capital city—Romero was appointed archbishop of San Salvador. At the time, he was widely regarded as a friend of the wealthy, who were largely indifferent to the country's widespread injustices. His election generated little hope and much suspicion among the Salvadoran people who had grown weary from seeking social vindication. But within six months of his tenure and to the surprise of most Salvadorans, Romero emerged as a defender of the poor and a prophet calling the whole nation to conversion. What accounted for this transformation?

Many of Romero's biographers identify the murder of his close friend, the Jesuit Father Rutilio Grande, as the catalyst for the archbishop's conversion. Father Grande had been working as pastor in Aguilares—a poor rural parish where peasants had organized into base communities and were now asking for fair wages and better working conditions. These demands angered the local landlords, who had Grande assassinated just two weeks after Romero's installation. But though Romero felt the tragic loss of his friend deeply, he never described this or any other event as effecting a "conversion." Instead, Romero spoke of his transformation as an evolution in his overall availability to God. Romero's reluctance to speak of "conversion" is fitting if we understand conversion not simply as a movement away from sin, but also as the Christian call to continually draw closer to God. Romero understood conversion as part and parcel of any authentic Christian life.

Before he became archbishop, Romero was widely known as a rigid traditionalist and often-taciturn priest. But nobody questioned his faith commitment—he was what people often call "a holy priest." Throughout most of his youth and for a large part of his adult life, Romero evinced an austere and even a scrupulous spirituality that focused on his personal relationship with Christ. In this, Romero's discipleship was exercised mainly by attending to the development of his interior life: prayer, devotions, and an array of ascetic practices. Although faithful to Church teaching, Romero was suspicious of any theology whose concern for social justice might lead to confrontation and conflict. He was kind and charitable to the poor, but their precarious situation did not seem to challenge his faith.

While it is impossible to know exactly what transpired in Romero's heart, it is clear that by the end of his first six months as archbishop he had undergone a profound spiritual transformation. I suggest that Romero's process of renewal began with his encounter with poor parishioners in Santiago de María and reached a turning point with Father Grande's death, becoming crystalized with his recognition of Christ's presence in the lives of the poor.

Romero himself described the first two episodes in a conversation that he had with the Jesuit Provincial of that time when they traveled together to Rome in 1979. Romero recounts that although he was born into a poor family, he distanced himself from such poverty when he entered the minor seminary at the age of thirteen. As time went on, his studies and his administrative work preoccupied most of his time and attention. He writes:

> They sent me to Santiago de María, and I ran into extreme poverty again. Those children were dying just because of the water they were drinking, those campesinos killing themselves in the harvest…you know, father, when a piece of charcoal has already been lit once, you do not have to blow on it much to get it to flame up….When I saw Rutilio dead, I thought, if they killed him for what he was doing, it is my job to go down the same road. So yes, I changed, but also came back home again.[1]

Romero's encounter with the poor slowly awakened him to their situation, drew him closer to them, and provided a new horizon that would help him discern the priorities for his future ministry.

Months later, the murder of Father Grande would become a tipping point in his personal and ministerial life. Theologian Jon Sobrino, who accompanied Romero to Aguilares after Grande's murder, recalls how shocked the archbishop was when he first saw Grande's lifeless body and how "hundreds of campesinos [stared] at him wondering what he was going to do about what had happened."[2] If Romero's experience in Santiago de María had kindled his love for the poor, it was Grande's death and his grieving community that lifted up the demands—and the possible cost—of such love.

As Romero began to incarnate himself more fully into the suffering that surrounded him, one can detect a shift in his spirituality as he rediscovered God in the midst of his suffering people. He articulated this insight three months after Grande's death, at which time the military had forcefully occupied the town of

Aguilares and killed dozens of peasants. Romero returned to the battered town to comfort and stand with its community, and in a homily he told the peasants gathered before him: "You are the image…of Christ, nailed to the cross."[3] This recognition of Christ's presence in the poor guided the remainder of Romero's life and episcopal ministry.

The experiences that culminated in Romero's encountering Christ crucified in the poor enabled him to reexamine his previous apprehensions and better integrate the content of his faith with the lived expression of it. Contemplation and action illuminated each other to converge in Romero's faithful response to Christ. This response, in turn, became concretized in his preferential love for the poor in whom Christ is radically present.

Thereafter Romero began to model an exemplary spirituality that confronted the demands of the Salvadoran reality through the following of a merciful Jesus who became poor *for us*. In Romero's words, "This is the commitment of being Christian: to follow Christ in the incarnation. If Christ, the God of majesty, became a lowly human and lived with the poor, and even died on a cross as slave, our Christian faith should also be lived in the same way. The Christian who does not want to live this commitment of solidarity with the poor is not worthy to be called Christian."[4]

This compassionate stance of solidarity informs all of Romero's later writings, preaching, and actions. It is from here that he called the Salvadoran Church to undergo the same process of conversion he had experienced to become a church *of* the poor. For him, the evangelizing mission of the church had to include both a pastoral response and a prophetic proclamation, both the struggle for structural transformation and the compassionate offering of forgiveness. Thus, Romero promoted the development of base communities. He sponsored institutions that offered the poor legal protection against unjust laws, and strongly defended people's right to organize. His Sunday homilies, which were the product of long hours of prayer, were surely the most important tool that Romero enlisted to incarnate God's word and evangelize his conflicted nation. With an ear to the *sensus fidelium* and with a spirit of participation never witnessed by the Salvadoran Church before, Romero gathered the input of theologians, social scientists, base communities, parishes, and popular organizations to explain and illuminate the events of the week in light of the Scriptures. His preaching denounced—with names, dates, and places—specific actions of injustice and repression while at the same time condemning the unjust socioeconomic structures and the ideology that perpetuated this poverty and violence.

Although partial to the poor, Romero never excluded the non-poor and instead called both poor and non-poor to conversion. His writings and his preaching make clear that he believed "there will be no true reconciliation between...people and God as long as there is no just distribution, as long as the goods of the earth in El Salvador are not for the benefit and happiness of all Salvadorans."[5] Despite this conviction, Romero consistently rejected violent solutions to the systemic injustice and always tempered his call for justice with a willingness to forgive. His compassion demonstrates that justice and forgiveness do not contradict one another, but are rather the Christian pillars of reconciliation. A day before his martyrdom, Romero preached, "There is no sin that remains unforgiven or enmity that cannot be reconciled as long as there is conversion and a sincere return to the Lord."[6]

In the end, Romero bore the consequence of following Jesus to the end in a conflicted world. In such a world, his practical love explains the reason for his death and illuminates, for us, the path of the resurrection. If Romero's faithfulness attests to a freedom that makes itself utterly available to God, his transformation testifies to a God who breaks through our limited conceptions of the divine to offer us new eyes, create us anew, and mission us as a church to recreate the world. Although an unfathomed mystery, Romero's God remains, across time and geography, reliably present and waiting for us in the other, the community, and especially in those who suffer. "The church," Romero still reminds us today, "would betray its own love for God and its fidelity to the gospel if it would stop being 'the voice of the voiceless,' a defender of the rights of the poor, a promoter of every just aspiration for liberation...to achieve a more just society, a society that prepares the way for the true Kingdom of God in history."[7]

HOMILIES

Let us not tire of preaching love;
it is the force that will overcome the world.
Let us not tire of preaching love.
Though we see that waves of violence
succeed in drowning the fire of Christian love,
love must win out; it is the only thing that can.[8]

We have never preached violence,
except the violence of love,
which left Christ nailed to a cross,
the violence that we must each do to ourselves
to overcome our selfishness
and such cruel inequalities among us.
The violence we preach is not the violence of the sword,
the violence of hatred.
It is the violence of love,
of brotherhood,
the violence that wills to beat weapons
into sickles for work.[9]

NOTES

1. María López Vigil, *Oscar Romero: Memories in Mosaic*, trans. Kathy Ogle (Washington, DC: EPICA, 2000), 158–59.

2. Jon Sobrino, *Archbishop Romero: Memories and Reflections*, trans. Robert R. Barr, (Maryknoll, NY: Orbis Books, 1990), 8.

3. Oscar Romero, Homily, June 17, 1977. http://www.sicsal.net/romero/homilias/C/index.html (accessed April 15, 2013).

4. Oscar Romero, *The Violence of Love*, comp. and trans. James R. Brockman (Farmington, Pa.: Plough Publishing House, 1998), 204.

5. Romero, *The Violence of Love*, 215.

6. Oscar Romero, Homily, March 23, 1980. http://www.sicsal.net/romero/homilias/C/index.html (accessed April 15, 2013).

7. Oscar Romero, *Voice of the Voiceless*, trans. Michael J. Walsh (Maryknoll, NY: Orbis Books, 2003), 138.

8. Oscar Romero, Homily, September 25, 1977. http://www.sicsal.net/romero/homilias/C/index.html.

9. Oscar Romero, Homily, November 27, 1977. http://www.sicsal.net/romero/homilias/C/index.html.

Dietrich Bonhoeffer

(1906–1945)

April 9

Dietrich Bonhoeffer was born in Breslau, Germany, in 1906. From an early age, Bonhoeffer displayed talent for music, which was important throughout his life. At the age of fourteen, he felt called to be a pastor. In 1927, Dietrich graduated from the University of Berlin with a doctorate in theology, and his thesis, *Sanctorum Communio* (Communion of Saints), became quite influential at the time. After graduating, he traveled through Spain and visited the United States. His travels broadened his theological outlook; he developed a more practical approach to interpreting the scriptures and became interested in social justice and ecumenism.

In 1931, Bonhoeffer returned to Berlin and was ordained a minister. This period was a time of great turmoil in Germany. The Weimar Republic was in upheaval. At the time of the Great Depression, there was widespread unemployment, one factor that led to the election of Hitler in 1933.

Apart from his theological writings, Bonhoeffer became known for his staunch resistance to the Nazi dictatorship. He opposed Hitler's philosophy and his persecution of Jews and felt that the Church had a responsibility to act against these policies.

Bonhoeffer formed a breakaway church, The Confessing Church, with Martin Niemoller, to oppose the Nazi-supported German Christian movement. However, practically speaking, it was difficult to find the best means to oppose this Nazification of society and church. Bonhoeffer felt disillusioned by the weakness of the opposition. In autumn 1933, he accepted a two-year appointment to a German-speaking Protestant Church in London. During this period, Bonhoeffer wrote many theological tomes, including *The Cost of Discipleship*, a study on the Sermon on the Mount, which called for greater spiritual discipline to gain "the costly grace."

Fear of being arrested caused Bonhoeffer to emigrate from Germany to the United States in June 1939. In less than two years, he returned to Germany, feeling remorse for not having the courage to practice what he preached. On his return, Bonhoeffer was denied the right to speak in public or publish any articles.

Bonhoeffer then joined the *Abwehr*, an organization that strongly opposed Hitler, and he was aware of various assassination plots to kill Hitler. During the darkest hours of the Second World War, Bonhoeffer began to question his own pacifism and saw the need for a violent opposition to a heinous regime. The *Abwehr* managed to help some German Jews escape to neutral Switzerland, and it was this involvement that led to Bonhoeffer's arrest in April 1943.

In the concentration camp, Bonhoeffer exhibited a deep spirituality by ministering to his fellow prisoners. Just twenty-three days before the German surrender, Bonhoeffer was executed by hanging in April 1945 while imprisoned at a Nazi concentration camp.

He remains an important symbol of opposition to Hitler, and his views on Christianity have become increasingly influential. The integration of his Christian faith and life and the international appeal of his writings have received broad recognition. Bonhoeffer is considered a theologian, whose theological reflections will inspire future generations of Christians to create a more spiritual and responsible millennium. Dietrich Bonhoeffer is one of the most famous theologians and martyrs of the twentieth century. His statue, one of ten modern martyrs, was unveiled in July 1998 and stands above the west entrance to Westminster Abbey, London.

DIETRICH BONHOEFFER

The Disciple

Anne Deneen

All of the extraordinary actions of Dietrich Bonhoeffer's life arose from his daily encounter in the word of God revealed in Jesus Christ. Even towards the end of his life, as he speculated in Tegel prison about a world where God seemed absent, he, nevertheless, with faith beyond faith, asserted, "In Jesus, God has said Yes and Amen to it all, and that Yes and Amen is the firm ground on which we stand."[1] For the Christian of the twenty-first century, Bonhoeffer's life bears witness to what he himself called the "cost of discipleship." His life and teachings offer an antidote to an increasingly secular Christianity, a development he foresaw, described, and sought to answer in his own thought and actions. In his reflections on discipleship, an essay first published in 1937, Bonhoeffer could have been prophesying the course of his own life. "Costly grace is the gospel which must be sought again and again, the gift which has to be asked for, the door at which one has to knock. It is costly, because it calls to discipleship; it is grace because it calls us to follow Jesus Christ. It is costly because it costs people their lives; it is grace because it thereby makes them live."[2] The costly treasure of gospel grace becomes a way of interpreting his life and death, just as Jesus Christ was, for Bonhoeffer, the central referent for existence.

Bonhoeffer's spiritual resistance to Nazism led to political resistance, which led to martyrdom. He understood Christian life as a participation in the life, ministry, passion, and resurrection of Jesus Christ, and all his work in pastoral care, ecumenism, ethics, political resistance, theology, and teaching demonstrates that understanding. He would not have understood his life as worthy of sainthood, apart from the paradoxical theological affirmation that every Christian is both saint and sinner.

Bonhoeffer's complete works, now in English, trace his spiritual development, as his reflections unfolded and matured as a young theologian, and then, as he was formed by the catastrophic turn in history toward war in the 1930s and early 1940s. During his early career as a pastor and theologian, Bonhoeffer served in Spain and England; he traveled widely, to Italy, Denmark, and the United States, studying and lecturing. In 1934, he was one of the founders of the anti-Hitler Confessing Church movement among German Protestant Churches. In 1939, he broke off his travels in the United States and returned to Germany. Following the line of costly grace, Bonhoeffer's own conscience led him to the decision. He wanted to be near to assist and accompany his family and friends in their experience of living under the Third Reich. He felt there would be no moral ground for him to stand on if he fled.

After his decision to return, he wrote Reinhold Neibuhr of his choice with what Neibuhr called "the finest logic of Christian martyrdom." "I shall have no right to participate in the reconstruction of Christian life in Germany after the war if I do not share the trials of this time with my people....Christians in Germany will face the terrible alternative of either willing the defeat of their nation in order that Christian civilization may survive, or willing the victory of their nation, thereby destroying our civilization. I know which of these alternatives I must choose, but I cannot make this choice in security."[3]

As a Lutheran, Bonhoeffer was deeply schooled in an understanding of Christian liberty where the Christian lives in the paradox of perfect freedom before God, and perfect servanthood toward the neighbor. Just as Christ was in Bonhoeffer's terms, the "man for others,"[4] so the Christian is a person for others, one whose life is lived in this world for the sake of others. In one of his last letters from prison, Bonhoeffer extended this understanding to ecclesiology. Early in his theological career, he had defined the Church as "Christ existing as community." He had a chance to test this understanding in his pastoral and theological work, in his travels, and as the director of the underground seminary of the Confessing Church at Finkenwalde.

Bonhoeffer's short, profound essay, *Life Together*, is the summation of his experiences of Christian community life at Finkenwalde. After the Gestapo closed the seminary, Bonhoeffer composed the text as a record of his ideas, with the help of his student, Eberhard Bethge. Bethge would become his dearest friend, editor, biographer, and relative by marriage. *Life Together* was written urgently in 1938, in four weeks, in the context of impending war and increased violence and the intensifying persecution of the German Jewish community.[5] If he could be said to have a "rule of life," this text is his "rule." Here, he lays down the spiritual foundation and practices of what we could call today "intentional" Christian community. In the seminary, he tested his hope for a vital communal life "under the Word;" that is, a common life shaped and directed by the scriptures. Bonhoeffer wanted to prepare pastors theologically for their preaching office, but also for a Christian community that would have the spiritual and moral strength to withstand the pressures facing a church under siege, pastors who would be called upon, as he was, as we all are, to name evil and to resist it.

In the opening paragraph of the first chapter, Bonhoeffer directs the reader to consider the cross, and the solitary Jesus who dies alone. Jesus came into the world for our sakes; so, too, Christian community must be lived in the world. Though Finkenwalde was underground, it was not a cloister. *Life Together* was to be understood as a life lived in the midst of the world, not in seclusion from the world. The Christian lives actively as an agent of grace in history, under the Word, in the light of the cross, for others. As Christ is the man for others, the Church is for others. In the summer of 1944, as he considered the status of the Church, his emerging ecclesiology reflected his Christology: "The church is the church only when it exists for others....The church must share in the secular problems of ordinary human life, not dominating but helping and serving. It must tell men of every calling what it means to live in Christ, to exist for others. In particular, our own church will have to take the field against the vices of *hubris*, power-worship, envy, and humbug, as the roots of all evil."[6]

Bonhoeffer's guidelines for common life are familiar to any Christian. They are based on baptismal promises and include spiritual reading, prayer, solitude and silence, community, the daily practice of forgiveness, an understanding and practice of receiving the sacraments, and service to the neighbor. Bonhoeffer powerfully asserts that Christian community is a "spiritual reality" created "only by the Holy Spirit." "Christian community means community through Jesus Christ and in Jesus Christ. There is no Christian community that is more than this, and none that is less than this. Whether it be a brief, single encounter or the daily community of many years, Christian community is solely this. We belong to one another only through and in Jesus Christ."[7] He is adamant on this point, yet because of this ground of spiritual reality, he saw the Church in terms of deep ecumenical union; that is, we are one because of Christ. That insight freed him to work in the ecumenical movements of his time. He saw the spiritual reality of Christian community as a basis for resistance, not only as confession, *status confessionis*,[8] but as a spiritual foundation for political action. The urgency of history demanded no less: tyranny, war, persecution of Jews, extermination. The foundation of this confessing, resisting community is "the clear, manifest word of God in Jesus Christ."[9]

Bonhoeffer immersed himself in the Scriptures. They were living words for him. He was a man who lived, as he put it, "under the Word." In his directions to his community of seminarians, he placed the Scriptures as central to their daily work. He saw the texts as an intertwined living whole in which Christians find their own story. The Scriptures offered knowledge of God, of salvation, and of comfort for the suffering. He kept a daily discipline of meditative contemplative reading; he wanted his community to recite psalms daily, in the communal offices, and in private. In prison, he continued his daily immersion in the Word. "What we call our life, our troubles, our guilt, and our deliverance are there in the Scriptures. Because it pleased God to act for us there, it is only there we will be helped. Only in the Holy Scriptures do we get to know our own story.…We must become acquainted with the Scriptures first and foremost for our salvation.…It is not our heart that determines our course, but God's Word."[10] He advocated a meditative practice of reading, ruminative and thorough, which reflected his own practice.

For Bonhoeffer, Christ as the "man of others" lived in this world, and his followers are people in and of the world. In prison, he began to understand "the profound this-worldliness of Christianity." In Tegel, on July 21, 1944, in the last year of his life, as he ruminated on his death, and the death around him, he wrote to Eberhard Bethge of a conversation he had once with a young French pastor. The two spoke of what they wanted to do. The young French pastor wanted to become a saint. Bonhoeffer said he wanted to learn faith.

> For a long time, I didn't realize the depth of that contrast. I thought I could acquire faith by living a holy life, or something like that.…I've discovered later, and I'm still discovering right up to this moment, that is only by living completely in this world that one learns to have faith. One must completely abandon any attempt to make something of oneself, whether it be a saint, or a converted sinner, or a churchman (a so-called priestly type!), a righteous man or an unrighteous one, a sick man or a healthy one. By this-worldliness I mean living unreservedly in life's duties, problems, successes and failures, experiences and perplexities. In so doing, we

> throw ourselves completely into the arms of God, taking seriously not our own sufferings, but those of God in the world—watching with Christ in Gethsemane. That, I think, is faith; that is *metanoia*....[11]

His final letters from prison include his most moving poems and prayers. One of them could be understood as his own eulogy. It is called "Who am I" and Bonhoeffer is deeply truthful about his own existence in it. He speaks of how others see him, as a gentle patient comforter of souls, whether prisoner or guard, and yet within, he struggles with restlessness, longing, freedom, yearning for the beauty of the world.

The poem's final lines speak his own self-understanding, and his life bears witness to their truth: "Who am I? They mock me, these lonely questions of mine. Whoever I am, thou knowest, O God, I am thine."[12]

PAULIST PRAYER FOR RECONCILIATION[13]

God of compassion,
You sent Jesus to proclaim a time of mercy
reaching out to those who had no voice,
releasing those trapped by their own shame,
and welcoming those scorned by society.

Make us ambassadors of reconciliation.
Open our ears that we may listen
with respect and understanding.
Touch our lips that we may speak
your words of peace and forgiveness.
Warm our hearts that we may bring
wholeness to the broken-hearted and
dissolve the barriers of division.

Guide the work of your Church
and renew us with the Spirit of your love.
Help us and all people shape a world
where all will have a place,
where the flames of hatred are quenched,
and where all can grow together as one.

Forgive, restore and strengthen us through
our Lord Jesus Christ. Amen.

NOTES

1. Dietrich Bonhoeffer, *Letters and Papers from Prison: The Enlarged Edition*, ed. Eberhard Bethge (New York: Touchstone, 1997), 391.

2. *Discipleship*, in Dietrich Bonhoeffer Works,Vol.4, English ed., eds. Geffrey B. Kelly and John D. Godsey (Minneapolis: Fortress, 2003), 45.

3. Qtd. by G. Leibholz, "Memoir," in *The Cost of Discipleship* (New York: Macmillan, 1963), 16.

4. Eberhard Bethge, in his magnificent biography of Dietrich Bonhoeffer, speaks of Bonhoeffer's "man for others" as a "Christological title of honor," original to Bonhoeffer, and is "confession, hymn, prayer and interpretation." *Dietrich Bonhoeffer: Man of Vision, Man of Courage* (New York: Harper and Row, 1977), 389.

5. For a riveting account of the history of the writing of *Life Together*, see Geffrey B. Kelly, "Editor's Introduction," in *Life Together/ Prayerbook of the Bible*, Dietrich Bonhoeffer Works, Vol.5, English ed., eds. Geffrey B. Kelly and John D. Godsey (Minneapolis: Fortress, 2005), 3–23.

6. *Letters and Papers*, 382–83.

7. *Life Together*, 31.

8. Eberhard Bethge, *Friendship and Resistance: Essays on Dietrich Bonhoeffer* (Geneva: WCC Publications, 1995), 25. "Today, Christians all over the world know that a *status confessionis* becomes rotten if it is limited to a confession *against* and does not go on to a confession *for*;

that is to say if the confessing Christian does not assume responsibility for society and its victims—in other words if it is not confession and resistance, confession accompanied by resistance."

9. *Life Together*, 39.
10. Ibid., 62–63.
11. *Letters and Papers*, 369–70.
12. Ibid., 348.
13. Prayer from Paulist Reconciliation Ministries, Washington, DC.

Philip Neri

(1515–1595)

May 26

Philip Neri was born in Florence in 1515, the youngest child of a noble family. He studied with the friars at San Marco, the Dominican monastery. At eighteen Philip was sent to work with an older cousin, a successful businessman in a small town near Naples. After a profound religious conversion, Philip left the business world and, in 1533, chose to relocate to Rome, where he worked as a live-in tutor. He pursued philosophy and theology until his studies were interfering with his prayer life. During one of these times of deep contemplative prayer, he felt a globe of light enter his mouth and sink into his heart. This experience gave him so much energy to serve God that he went out to work at the hospital of the incurables.

In 1548, Philip formed a confraternity with other laymen to minister to pilgrims who came to Rome without food or shelter. The director convinced Philip that he could be more effective as a priest. After receiving priestly training, Philip was ordained in 1551.

He settled down with some companions at the hospital of San Girolamo della Carità, and while there he began the institute called the Oratory in 1556. The format was a series of evening meetings in a hall (the Oratory), at which there were prayers, hymns, readings from Scripture, the Church fathers, and the Martyrology, followed by a lecture. The members of the society also did mission work throughout Rome, especially preaching in different churches every evening, an innovative concept at that time.

Under papal permission, Philip formally organized a community of secular priests and clerics called the Congregation of the Oratory in 1575. In the Oratory, the laity are first and the priests and brothers exist to serve the laity, who are therefore rightly the first order. Noted for seeking to reform the Church from within and to restore Rome and the Vatican to a life of charity and prayer, Philip brought democratic ideas to the practice of Catholicism. Neri encouraged the singing of the *lauda spirituale* (lauds) in his oratory services. The composers Tomás Luis de Victoria and Giovanni Pierluigi da Palestrina contributed their music to the gatherings. The Oratory spread chiefly in Italy and in France, where by 1760 there were fifty-eight houses all under the government of a superior-general.

Very serious about prayer, Philip often became rapt for hours in deep contemplation. When asked how to pray, he replied, "Be humble and obedient and the Holy Spirit will teach you." Combined with his extraordinary popularity, Philip's piety won over many in Rome's corrupt society. He possessed a playful humor and a shrewd wit, and he was known to be spontaneous, unpredictable, and charming.

Renowned for his outstanding personal love for Christ, Philip died at the age of eighty in 1595 after a long illness. St. Philip Neri was beatified by Pope Paul V in 1615, and canonized by Pope Gregory XV in 1622. His memorial is celebrated on May 26. Philip Neri is patron saint of Rome and of joy; his body rests in the *Chiesa Nuova* (the New Church) in Rome. The second largest Catholic Church in London is the well-known Oratorian Church of the Immaculate Heart of Mary, built in Brompton and consecrated in 1884.

PHILIP NERI

"The Fire of Joy"

Michael McGarry, CSP

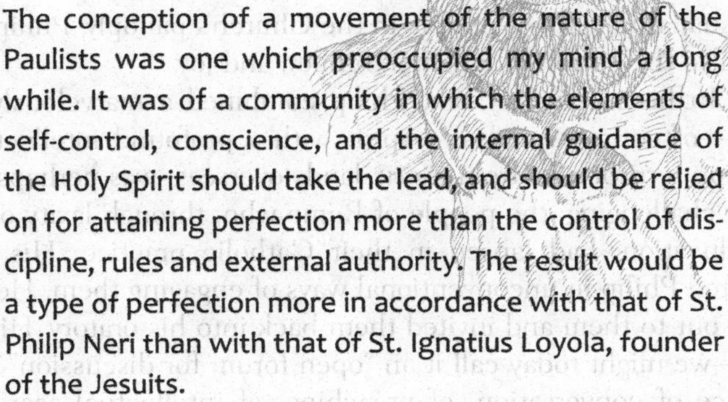

> **The conception of a movement of the nature of the Paulists was one which preoccupied my mind a long while. It was of a community in which the elements of self-control, conscience, and the internal guidance of the Holy Spirit should take the lead, and should be relied on for attaining perfection more than the control of discipline, rules and external authority. The result would be a type of perfection more in accordance with that of St. Philip Neri than with that of St. Ignatius Loyola, founder of the Jesuits.**
>
> **Servant of God, Isaac Thomas Hecker**[1]

When he imagined a movement on fire with the zeal of St. Paul, Servant of God Isaac Thomas Hecker dreamt large for a small group of men. He never thought that the Paulists should be great in number; indeed, he feared losing quality for the price of large numbers. Hecker wanted this small band to gain their strength from their natural abilities and the personal inspiration of the Holy Spirit.

Who would inspire such a group?

Like a lighthouse beam that sweeps over the historical array of great Christian lives, Hecker looked for candidates—saints—

who would both inspire and model the Paulist missionary. Of course, he admired the great founders of religious orders, like Francis, Dominic, and Ignatius. But Hecker zeroed in on others who, from his perspective, exemplified better his Paulist ideal, beginning of course with St. Paul. Taking the twin reference points of the candidate's "zeal for souls" and his commitment to "personal perfection," Hecker found another such model in St. Philip Neri. As he said, the Paulists will find "a type of perfection more in accordance with that of St. Philip Neri…"

But who was this sixteenth-century priest founder of the Oratorians who so inspired Isaac Hecker? The titles of biographies about Philip Neri offer convenient glimpses into the man: he was "the Fire of Joy," "the Apostle of Rome," the "Roman Socrates." Unusual although not unique in the Church's panoply, Philip Neri was also the patron of laughter, humor, and joy.

In his missionary life, Philip combined a marvelously creative—oftentimes puckish—spirit with a profound intellect. His mission territory, far from exotic lands overseas, was perhaps even more challenging: the people of Rome who, through laxity or lack of education, had lapsed in their Catholic practice. His mind inspired Philip in unconventional ways of engaging them. He both went out to them and invited them back into his oratory. His oratory—we might today call it an "open forum for discussion"—was a place of conversation, of preaching, of intellectual searching, and of prayer. It was a precursor, we might even say, to today's "theology-on-tap" discussion forums.

With imagination and not infrequently "stick-it-in-your-eye" humor, often bordering on the absurd, Philip approached folks who were already baptized Christians, almost all of them Catholics, and presented the faith in ways that were both intellectually stimulating and personally enriching. Watching for even the coolest embers of faith, Philip Neri also thought of new ways to blow on those embers in order to reignite them.

Philip was also revered for his unabashed, almost limitless, faith in the personal promptings of the Holy Spirit. He contrasted his community from more organized and structured groups like the Franciscans and Dominicans. It is no wonder, then, that when Isaac Hecker, not long after his experience at Fruitlands, where free thought and rational inquiry were championed, found in Philip Neri and his Oratorians a schema for his own congregation. Hecker thought of his congregation as a *movement*, thus reflecting the dynamic character of his dream.

Always returning to the anchor of a life immersed in a strong, indeed contemplative prayer life, both Philip Neri and Hecker thought that otherwise useful ecclesial structures sometimes constricted rather than unleashed their respective movements' energy. In a way that made up for external structures, both Philip and Hecker insisted on grounding their mission in intense, personal prayer. Like a boat with its sails set taut for the westward wind, Hecker's company would catch the Spirit's breath in their prayer to propel them as their zealous energy. The Spirit would empower their imagination; it would stoke their perseverance to go out, again and again, to preach the good news of Jesus Christ. For Philip Neri, the Spirit pushed him into the Roman streets; for Isaac Thomas Hecker that same Spirit pushed him to bring the good news of Jesus Christ and his Church into the American people and culture.

Hecker found in Philip Neri a saint who was a "natural fit" to inspire his missionaries. The danger, however, as with many saints, is that Christians end up *admiring* their saints rather than *imitating* them.

I remember well the awkward but telling moment when an IBM personnel manager confronted me after my particularly eloquent (I thought) homily on Mother Teresa. She challenged me: "I work as a personnel manager at IBM—*I am not* Mother Teresa." The trick in modeling ourselves after the great saints, of course, is *translation*: how can we translate Mother Teresa's sanctity into the life of a personnel director at IBM? While the world might be improved by having more Mother Teresas, it may be even better to have saints working at IBM. As a matter of fact, most Christians go to school or work in a business or at a hospital or on a construction site, or we take care of an elderly relative. Unique saints like Francis or Mother Teresa can be too distant. We admire them, but tomorrow the alarm clock will ring at 6:00 a.m. and we're on the bus by 7:15 a.m. for another day. The danger of saints is that we keep them so distant that all we can do is admire them, or they are so impossible to imitate that we leave ourselves feeling simply guilty or inadequate.

Philip Neri, although a singularly inventive and tireless apostle to Rome, is wonderfully translatable for us who live lives out in the world and have obligations to family and community. What can we followers of Hecker draw from the extraordinary but singular life of Philip Neri that can actually inform our own following of Jesus?

I would suggest three special dimensions of Philip Neri's sanctity that we ordinary Christians can imitate: *joy, ingenuity* (intelligence joined with cleverness), and *attention to the inner workings of the Holy Spirit*. Hecker wanted these for his movement, and we can translate them into our daily lives.

We claim that we are the resurrection people. We believe passionately in the life, death, and resurrection of Jesus of Nazareth, and we see therein the promise of our own future. But to meet some Christians, one might wonder if they had swallowed too much castor oil in their lives—what was the word we used when we were children? "Sourpuss!" But Jesus' follower's life is one of joy. As one of my Paulist colleagues bluntly put it: "You say you believe in the Resurrection? Inform your face!" Philip Neri attracted people back to the Church in Rome with his infectious and never-to-be discouraged joyful personality. He had *informed his face*! In fact, his face could not but reflect the deep joy that was his. No wonder he was so successful in attracting wandering Christians back to the Church.

Secondly, Philip Neri had that special gift to inject his considerable intellect (many people have intelligence—not as many have the cleverness to bridge to others' intellects) into a wit that deflates pomposity and sanctimony. This is ingenuity. For example, when one of his followers reveled in his own preaching expertise, Philip required that the priest repeat the same sermon six times so that others would think he only had one sermon. That certainly deflated his ego! When another follower tried to display his superior sanctity by wearing a penitential hair shirt, Philip insisted that this enthusiast wear the hair shirt *on the outside* of his clothes to draw laughter rather than admiration as a gentle "putting in his place." Philip was delightfully unpredictable in his interactions with people, winning them over more often by good humor and cleverness than by pounding them with crushing rational arguments.

Thirdly, Hecker was attracted by Philip Neri's commitment to a strong prayer life that abided many hours in contemplation. As paradoxical as it sounds, both Hecker and Philip realized that an active band of men depended more on the personal inspiration of the Holy Spirit than on external rules—and this required *more discipline* rather than less. The kind of missionary work that Hecker wanted for his troops required men on fire with love for God, for their fellows, and for their country. It required that, in love, they engaged the world rather than retreated from it into safe, "pure" havens. Even today, some Church voices, like Cassandra, keep talking about the evils of the world and how we must combat those evils by removing ourselves into sheltered caves of sectarian exclusiveness. But for the God who sent his only Son *into the world* because He *loved the world*, this will never do. Make no mistake, though: there is indeed a danger of being drawn into a worldliness—as pervaded in Philip's world of ecclesiastical corruption and laxity—that is as seductive as it is comfortable. To find the right attenuation is no easy feat. And the only way to find that place is returning on a daily basis to a deep prayer life. Philip Neri recognized this and practiced it.

Indeed, it is not surprising that Hecker found in Philip Neri one source of inspiration for his movement. So too can we find in this joyful, playful, but entirely grounded saint an inspiration for our own lives. And we can *imitate* him as well as admire him. What a marvelous saint!

LITANY FOR ST. PHILIP NERI[2]

Lord, have mercy on us.
Christ, have mercy on us.
Lord, have mercy on us.
Christ, hear us.
Christ, graciously hear us.
God the Father of Heaven, have mercy on us.
God the Son, Redeemer of the world, have mercy on us.
God the Holy Spirit, have mercy on us.
Holy Trinity, One God, have mercy on us.
Holy Mary, Mother of God, have mercy on us.

(Response: have mercy on us)

Saint Philip Neri,
Vessel of the Holy Spirit,
Apostle of Rome,
Counsellor of popes,
Voice of prophecy,
Joyful proclaimer of Christ's love,
Man of primitive times,
Winning saint,
Hidden hero,
Flower of purity,
Mediator of mercy through confession,
Jester of God's compassion,
Tamer of proud hearts,
Martyr of charity,
Heart of fire,
Discerner of spirits,
Mirror of the divine life,
Pattern of humility,
Example of simplicity,
Light of holy joy,

Image of childhood,
Picture of old age,
Director of souls,
Gentle guide of youth,

Saint Philip Neri
You received the Holy Spirit into your heart,
You experienced such wonderful ecstasies,
You so lovingly served the little ones,
You washed the feet of pilgrims,
You distributed the daily word of God,
You turned so many hearts to God,
You set up your houses in all lands,

Christ, hear us.
Christ, graciously hear us.

Let us pray.
Loving God, Who has exalted Saint Philip, Your confessor,
in the glory of Your saints, grant that,
as we rejoice in his commemoration,
so may we profit by the example of his virtues,
through Christ Our Lord. Amen.

NOTES

1. *Paulist Prayer Book*, 127.
2. Adapted from the Litany by John Henry Cardinal Newman.

MARY OF MAGDALA

July 22

Mary of Magdala traveled with Jesus as one of his women disciples and followers. They stayed with him at the cross after most of the male disciples had fled. Mary of Magdala stood at the foot of the cross, supporting him in his final moments with his Mother Mary, as she mourned his death. She was also present at the anointing of his body and at his burial. Mary of Magdala is the *apostle to the apostles*, the one who found the empty tomb and the first to see Jesus raised from the dead and to proclaim his resurrection to the other disciples.

Mary of Magdala is perhaps the most misunderstood and maligned figure in early Christianity. In Christian art and hagiography, Mary has been romanticized beyond recognition. Since the fourth century, she has been portrayed as a prostitute and public sinner who, after encountering Jesus, repented and spent the rest of her life in penitence. Yet the actual biblical account of Mary of Magdala is very different. Scripture portrays her as the primary witness to the most central events of Christian faith in each of four

Gospels. It is impossible to relate the story of the resurrection without including "Mary, the one from Magdala." The twenty-first century has seen a restoration of Mary of Magdala as the patron saint of women's ministry.

Her feast day is July 22. The Eastern Orthodox churches also commemorate her on the Sunday of the Myrrh-bearers, the Orthodox equivalent of the Western Three Marys.

MARY OF MAGDALA

Apostle of Apostles

Mary R. D'Angelo

> "She was glorified by his first appearance; raised up to the honor of an apostle; instituted as the evangelist of the resurrection of Christ; and designated the prophet of his ascension to his apostles."[1]
>
> "Tell us, Mary, say what you saw on the way."[2]

In the words of Jane Schaberg, Mary Magdalene has experienced a resurrection in recent years, emerging as a saint for our time.[3] She has had a strange career in Christian history and imagination. While Western Christians often thought of her primarily as a repentant prostitute, she is now recognized by the ancient title *apostola apostolorum*: apostle of apostles. In recent years, scholarly and feminist readings of the New Testament, seeking in part to rethink the ways women participated in the early church, have returned to the Gospel sources and investigated rediscovered texts from the early centuries.

Mary of Magdala is an important figure in the Gospels, yet they give us mystifyingly little information about her. In Mark and Matthew, she heads the list of (named and unnamed) women who were the last disciples to follow Jesus from afar to his death and burial (Mark 15:40–47; Matt 27:55, 66; cf. Luke 23:49). In John, she appears at the cross in the company of Jesus' mother and aunt (19:25). With other women, she is the first witness to the empty tomb and the messenger of the resurrection (Mark 16:1–8; Matt 28:1–8; Luke 24:10). She alone is John's first witness to the empty tomb and the first to see the risen Jesus in that Gospel (20:1–18; also in the appendix to Mark, printed as 16:9–20). Matthew credits her (and "the other Mary" 28:9–10) with the first vision of the risen Jesus. Luke introduces her at the head of a list of women disciples at an earlier point in the narrative. In Luke's version, these women were patrons who supported preachers of God's reign, and came to be disciples because they were cured of diseases or demonic possession. Mary, the most famous of them, had been the most afflicted; according to Luke she had been possessed by seven devils (8:1–3).

In all the canonical Gospels, Mary is the first witness to the resurrection. Where a list of women disciples is given, she always comes first. The name, Magdalene, seems to come not from a parent, husband, child, or sibling, but from her town of origin, as Jesus is called "Nazarene" or "of Nazareth." Magdala's Greek name was Tarichaea. Because it was known for exporting dried fish, some scholars have speculated on Mary's work. Was she a wealthy owner of boats, or a producer of dried fish? Did she actually fish herself? Was she a poor woman attracted by the hope of justice in God's reign? At any rate, the parallel between her name and Jesus' suggests that she was a leader in the reign-of-God movement before his death as well as in the missionary movement that was driven by the resurrection.

Only John gives Mary a speaking role. She is clear-sighted and persistent in the midst of her grief and three times draws the logical conclusion from the empty tomb: grave robbers (John 20:2, 13, 15). Once Jesus speaks to her, she knows him and is equally insistent about what she has seen and heard: "I have seen the Lord," she says, and passes on the message he has given her (20:17–18). This scene makes clear how Mary gained the title *apostle*. She can present the same credentials by which Paul defended his apostleship: she had a vision of the risen Lord (20:18; see 1 Cor 9:1); she was sent to proclaim a message (John 20:17; see 1 Cor 1:17); and that message was the foundation of a community (John 20:17; see 1 Cor 9:1).[4]

In texts of the second century once lost or labeled *gnostic*, Mary appears among the other disciples, asking questions of Jesus and responding to his speeches (*Gospel of Thomas* 21, *Dialogue of the Savior*, *Pistis Sophia*). The *Gospel of Philip* speaks of her as Jesus' partner or companion. The *Gospel of Mary* portrays her as visionary and leader of the disciples after the resurrection, relating the revelation given to her and encouraging the others to take up the mission of preaching the gospel. When Peter and Andrew object to her revelation's content and her female status, she is vindicated by Levi who recalls the charge to preach the gospel, making no other rule or law. The *Gospel of Thomas* similarly reflects tensions over women and salvation from the second century (114).

The third-century writer Hippolytus is the first known to have used the title *apostola apostolorum* of the women at the tomb; he describes them as sent by Christ, and declares that in them, Eve has become an apostle (*Commentary on the Songs of Songs* 25). The title was frequently repeated by Christian writers, such as the ancient scripture scholar St. Jerome. At the same time, Western writers began seeking more information about so important a saint. They created a biography for Mary Magdalene by identifying her with Mary of Bethany (sister of Martha, John 11:1—12:11 and Luke 10:38–42), and combined both women with the repentant sinner who anoints Jesus' feet in Luke 7:35–50. From this combination arose the tradition that Mary Magdalene must have been a prostitute. In the Middle Ages, seeing Mary as a repentant prostitute did not so much obscure her role as witness and apostle as make it more impressive. One medieval miniature depicts her preaching to the disciples, and she was supplied with a long and far-ranging missionary career preaching the gospel to the West, as far as France. In the West, the Easter liturgy preserved the memory of Mary as first witness to the resurrection. But art and piety after the Renaissance increasingly envisioned her as a penitent, and most paintings focused on the glorious hair that identified her with the repentant sinner.

Eastern Christians never combined the two Marys and the woman penitent, but focus on her witness to the resurrection. The Orthodox churches celebrate her as Myrrh-bearer and Apostle-Equal on two feast days: one on July 22, for her alone, and also on the Third Sunday of Pascha, Sunday of the holy Myrrh-bearers. A legend developed in Ephesus that Mary preached to the emperor Tiberius, who said he would believe in resurrection when the egg she was holding up as an example of rebirth turned red—and it did. This legend is the basis of a number of recently painted icons.[5]

The Sequence for Easter entreats, "Tell us, Mary, what you saw on the way." What do Mary and her history have to tell us? It's easy to hear her message of persistent and clear-sighted hope, and to see her as example both in her search for Jesus' body and in her commitment to her message. But there are important ways in which looking with Mary enables us to see new realities in the ancient and contemporary Church.

First, hearing from Mary means rehearing her message. It's essential not only to realize that the good news of the resurrection offered hope to the disciples but also to rehear the message the resurrection affirmed, the message that Jesus preached and that she heard and took up herself: "The time is fulfilled, God's reign is come near" (Mark 1:15; cp. Matt 10:7 and Luke 10:9, 11). For Mary, as for other Jews of her time, God's kingdom, God's reign meant a new world order. When God reigns, the poor reign, the hungry are filled, the humble are lifted up, those who weep receive comfort, and there is freedom to worship without fear, in holiness and justice before God always (Luke 6:20, 21; 1:52–53, 75). To rehear Mary is to commit to an order of greater justice, especially justice for the poor.

Second, resurrecting Mary of Magdala changes our vision of the beginning of Christianity by repopulating it with women. Distinguishing Mary of Magdala, Mary of Bethany, and the woman of Luke 7:35–50 as three separate women casts Mary's role as witness and apostle into high relief, and at the same time, uncovers more women in Christianity's foundations. And there are many more to retrieve: the other women witnesses to the resurrection, who share her apostolic title (Mary of James and Joses, Salome, Johanna); Mary and Martha, and the many unnamed women of the Gospels; Junia the apostle, the missionary partner and perhaps spouse of Andronicus (Rom 16:7); Phoebe the *diakonos*, or minister (Rom 16:1–12); Prisca, Mary, Persis, Tryphaena and Tryphosa, and Julia, all workers in the Roman mission before Paul (Rom 16:3–15), and many others, named and unnamed. Relocating Mary in this new, more diverse and crowded picture of the creators of Christianity should lead us to a more just recognition of the Spirit at work in the women of the contemporary Church.

Third, recognizing that Mary was mislabeled as a prostitute should cause Christians to rethink the sexual suspicion that shadows women, especially young women. The "Magdalene Laundries" offer an extreme example of the damage this suspicion has done. Girls who were convicted or suspected of prostitution, who had been raped, who were single mothers, or who were seen as potentially "falling" were labeled "Magdalenes" and subjected to unpaid labor as penance, with the collusion of the Church, of the Irish government, and often of their own families. Rethinking Mary Magdalene should cause us to fear defining women and men as sexual outlaws, and to seek just power relations in all intimate exchanges, and especially in the economic arrangements behind sex work.

The new Mary—actually, the old, original Mary—is now remembered for her vision and her voice. What she saw and what she says are the basis of our faith: she is witness to the transformation from death to life. The "new look" at Mary Magdalene is only a beginning; surely she has more to tell us, more to set us on new ways. Tell us, Mary.

PRAYER TO MARY OF MAGDALA[6]

Holy Mary of Magdala,
You followed our Lord Jesus faithfully
In his earthly ministry and were first

To witness to his glorious resurrection.
Standing with his mother at the cross,
You shared the pain of mother and son
And felt with them the joy of his risen life.

Apostle to the apostles,
With all your women companions
Pray that we, too, will serve Christ faithfully,
Embrace his cross with generosity,
And rejoice with him in the company
Of all his saints in heaven. Amen.

Mary of Magdala, apostle of apostles, pray for us.

NOTES

1. Chap. 29, lines 1665–70, translated by David Mycoff, in *The Life of Saint Mary Magdalene and of her Sister Saint Martha*; Cistercian Studies 168 (Kalamazoo: Cistercian Publications, 1989), 79. This *Life* (one of many medieval lives) appears to date from the late twelfth century (Mycoff 10).

2. This translation is my own, as are all others not explicitly acknowledged.

3. *The Resurrection of Mary Magdalene: Legends, Apocrypha and the Christian Testament* (New York: Continuum, 2002).

4. D'Angelo, "Reconstructing Real Women from Gospel Literature: the Case of Mary Magdalene," *Women in Christian Origins*; ed. R. S. Kraemer and M. R. D'Angelo (New York: Oxford University Press, 1999), 105–28.

5. Bruce Chilton, *Mary Magdalene: A Biography* (New York: Doubleday, 2005), 2.

6. Composed by Suzanne Beebe. Used by permission.

Ignatius Loyola

(1491–1556)

July 31

Inigo de Loyola, the founder of the Society of Jesus, the Jesuits, was born at the family castle in Loyola, Spain in 1491. Following the family tradition, he became a soldier in 1521 and was seriously wounded in battle in Pamplona. During his lengthy convalescence at home, he read the life of Christ and the lives of many saints and had a conversion to the faith. With the same determination that he brought to his military service, he now turned to his re-found Catholic faith.

Over the years, Ignatius became expert in the art of spiritual direction. He collected his insights, prayers, and suggestions in his book the *Spiritual Exercises,* one of the most influential books on the spiritual life ever written.[1] As a guide to spiritual growth, his work received wide approval and was used by clergy and lay from its first edition to today.

Ignatius was ordained a priest in 1537. With a small group of friends, he founded the Society of Jesus, or the Jesuits. Ignatius conceived the Jesuits as "contemplatives in action." This also describes the many Christians who have been touched by Ignatian spirituality.[2] He and his first followers offered their lives and service to Pope Paul III who gave approval to the new Society of Jesus in 1540. The following year he was elected the first general of the Jesuits. He founded the Roman College, now the Pontifical Gregorian University in Rome.

Ignatius died in Rome on July 31, 1556. He was beatified in 1609 and was enrolled in the calendar of saints on March 12, 1622.

NOTES

1. Cf. Ignatianspirituality.com
2. Ibid.

IGNATIUS LOYOLA

Living in the Company of Jesus

John Randall Sachs, SJ

For over four hundred years, the *Spiritual Exercises* of Ignatius have been a source of renewal for countless Christian women and men. The Ignatian vision they embody offers many helpful insights for spirituality today. I would like to reflect on three.

1. *God creates the cosmos out of love and calls each one of us to play a creative part in its development*. Ignatius began his *Spiritual Exercises* with what he called the *Principle and Foundation*: we believe that God creates the entire cosmos completely out of love in order to share God's love and life with it, in every human being (*SpEx* 23). God is personally present, desiring to touch every heart, revealing in some way God's gracious and saving love, and calling us to live in it more deeply. God's creative action is not just "in the beginning." At every instant, God is loving the cosmos and all its creatures into existence. Our world is part of God's "work-in-progress," a creative labor that God calls us to be a part of. The final salvation that God desires is not meant just for human beings but for God's whole creation (Rom 8). Nonetheless, made as an image of God, each person is uniquely equipped with freedom and imagination to share in and show forth God's own divine life and creativity in his or her own distinctive way. For this

reason, Ignatius understood that God's will for each individual is not only a question of fidelity to traditional principles and practices of holy living. It is a call rooted in the unique traits, strengths, weaknesses, and personal history of each person that elicits a free and imaginative response. There may be moments when one hears God's call in a unique or extraordinary way, but from an Ignatian perspective, God is already "speaking" to us in all the particular characteristics that make us who we are.

Ignatius realized that we can only respond authentically if our freedom is truly freed in Christ and our creative imagination remains rooted in and in tune with God's loving and empowering Spirit. Although noted for the way he esteemed obedience, he was convinced that God's will and purpose is not to subdue human freedom, but to activate and energize it, setting it free *from* the forces of sin and death that threaten it *for* a life of love, creativity, and service. As St. Irenaeus wrote: "The glory of God is the human person fully alive." This is how we should understand the meaning of Ignatius's famous prayer, the *Suscipe* (*SpEx* 234).

Ignatius knew from experience how difficult it is to become truly free. It is a lifelong process. But because God's love is unconditional—a free gift and not a reward for our good deeds—we can have confidence and courage to be real with God. I can admit my own sinfulness and pay attention to those areas in which I am not free, where my desire and use of things, or the way I treat people, show that it's still "all about me." I can rely on God for the grace of ongoing conversion, forgiveness, and healing. Such conversion entails a reordering of priorities: one should not prefer wealth over poverty, health over sickness, fame over disgrace, but rather, in whatever circumstance, one should strive to love, to share, and to serve as fully as one can for the *greater glory of God*. For Ignatius, this is what it means to know that I am a sinner who is loved by God and called to trust in the power of God's love to lead me to true freedom and more authentic human living.

2. *Christ calls us into a relationship of love and labor with him in service of the reign of God*. Ignatius's own conversion involved a

great reversal of fortune and priorities. His previous quest for honor in the service of the king seemed empty compared to the new desire he felt to serve God like the great saints did. In La Storta, just outside Rome, Ignatius had a profound experience of God placing him in the company of Christ his Son carrying the cross. In the second week of the *Exercises*, Ignatius encourages people to consider in what particular way Christ the King might be calling them into such a relationship. Every believer is called to become a friend and companion of Christ in some way (*SpEx* 91–98).

To this end, he proposed a helpful way of praying by contemplating the Gospel scenes of Christ's life. After slowly reading a passage once or twice, he encouraged one to use one's imagination and senses, picturing the scene and considering what Christ says and does. In him, we see what God's reign is all about, what God is doing so that the world will finally become what he wants it to be. Christ reveals that God's truth and justice are a love deeper and a mercy wider than we expect or imagine possible—embracing everyone. Jesus reveals the presence and promise of God's reign *and* its demands in real, everyday living.

After praying this way with scripture, one then takes some time to reflect on what happened. How did I imagine the scene? What was Jesus like? How did people respond to him? How did I respond? What did I feel? Did any desires or fears arise within me? Over the years, Ignatius had become confident that such affective movements of the heart are important ways in which one can discover how Christ may be calling one to intimate companionship and friendship with him. One can discover, too, the ways one might feel resistance or fear as one considers responding in some way to that invitation. Such self-awareness is important, especially so that one might ask the Lord for the particular grace that one needs and desires to receive from him. For Ignatius, that grace was to know Christ more intimately, so that he might love *and* follow him more wholeheartedly in service of God's reign (*SpEx* 104). As is true in any mature relationship, an authentic spirituality is not only about Jesus and me loving each other; it is about the gift of that shared love flowing outward in loving service of others.

Spending time this way with Christ, we might find ourselves, like Ignatius, drawn to him, touched more deeply by his love and his vision of the Kingdom. As I marvel at God's ever-greater love in action—a love that leaves no one out—I may find my love for Christ growing, feeling a desire to be with him at a deeper level, to be more like him in the way he is able to love and serve. Sometimes the love of another brings out the best in you! This was Ignatius's experience, and it is summed up in the Jesuit motto: in everything, strive to do what is *for the greater glory of God* (often abbreviated AMDG for the Latin, *Ad Majorem Dei Gloriam*).

Although Ignatius's love for Christ and desire to imitate him in all things—especially in his poverty, humility, and suffering—originally expressed itself in the practice of extreme penances and drew him to the Holy Land, he came to see that following Christ did not mean trying to imitate him literally, but being poised and ready in ever-new circumstances to respond to the call of Christ and the reign of God in new and creative ways. When he prayed, "Take, Lord, and receive all my liberty; my memory, understanding, my entire will," he was not asking God to remove his freedom and imagination but to transform, shape, and energize them in the Spirit. The one who follows Christ wholeheartedly will find in the Spirit, plenty of room for authentic, individual improvisation.

3. *Being a companion of Christ means being a contemplative in action*. At that time what made the new Jesuit order different from others, which were either contemplative or active, was Ignatius's desire to combine both: to bring the depth of monastic life into the breadth of life in the world. This is why he considered it essential that its members be *contemplatives in action*. The Ignatian approach to contemplative living and praying in the world has much to offer us all today.

Although Ignatius himself was one of the great mystics of the Church, the contemplative prayer and attitude he recommends is more like a simple habit of paying attention. It means keeping one's eyes and heart open to Christ in the scripture, to the movements of God's Spirit in the desires of one's heart, to the wonders of God's creation, and to the needs of the world. God calls each of us to this kind of contemplation: paying attention in order to recognize God's presence and to stay in tune with God's action in the world.

There are many helpful ways to develop a contemplative attitude. In a wonderful poem entitled "The Summer Day," Mary Oliver writes: "I don't know exactly what a prayer is. / I do know how to pay attention." Her poems are born of a deep and loving attentiveness to the world of nature, something for which Ignatius, too, was well known. Many people find that through her poems, their own eyes and hearts are opened up prayerfully to a deeper awareness of self, the world, the presence of God, and into a more contemplative way of living.

If one takes the time to pay attention, one can experience the presence and action of God as Spirit in the mysteries and miracles of everyday human living: faithful love, a friendship in which I discover myself in a new way: the birth of a child, being forgiven, being able to forgive, overcoming an addiction, the courage to do the right thing in a difficult situation, the unexpected strength to endure sickness or suffering—these and many more.

We are called to pay attention to how God is present in and with the poor, the suffering and the victims of injustice, for we believe that Christ has identified himself in a special way with them (Matt 25). We are called to see them the way God does. From an Ignatian perspective, desiring to do what is "for the greater glory of God" draws us with Christ into God's own "preferential option for the poor." In the second week of the *Spiritual Exercises*, Ignatius proposes that one imagine how God, looking down upon the earth and seeing its sin and suffering, decides to become human in order to save it (*SpEx* 102). In the company of Christ we, too, shall find ourselves seeing the world in a different way. The theologian Johann Baptist Metz writes that Jesus taught a "mysticism of open eyes...that especially makes visible all invisible and inconvenient suffering, and—convenient or not—pays attention to it and takes responsibility for it, for the sake of a God who is a friend to human beings." The theologian and poet Dorothee Sölle also speaks of a "mysticism of wide-open eyes," which unites one with God so that one "sees the world with God's eyes" and becomes one with God in responding to what one sees.

In this sense, contemplation leads to, and is actually transformed into, action. As companions of the risen Jesus, we are not mere spectators of his action, but find ourselves called and drawn into it. While we all need periods of quiet withdrawal and replenishment, the goal of Ignatian contemplation and the active spirituality it nurtures is not simply to calm down and chill out, but to remain in tune with Christ, who is still laboring in the world to bring about the fullness of God's reign. Such contemplation requires that one develop habits of praying and acting that help one pay better attention to Christ and the values of God's reign, and to become better informed about the world and its needs. This will help us to see where we are still living only on the surface of things and lead us to the real depths, to what is really important. It can help us to learn how to pay better attention to God's world and its suffering, to see the world as Christ does, and open our eyes to the ways the living Christ still wishes to act in the world through us.

In addition to regular periods of silence and occasional retreats, one particularly helpful and well-known Ignatian form of prayer called the Examination of Consciousness (or the *Examen*) is helpful. It is a daily practice of paying attention to how God has been a part of one's day. Take five or ten minutes of quiet time and ask Jesus to be with you as you reflect on the events of the day. Which ones were significant? What are the blessings for which you are grateful? Where was there darkness, difficulty, or suffering? When did you experience God's closeness; when may you have missed or turned away from God's loving presence? When did you feel more alive, more "in sync" with God, with others, with yourself? When not? As you conclude, tell Jesus about the desires, cares, or fears in your heart, and ask for what you desire. Becoming human in Jesus, God has invited each of us into an adult relationship of love in which one can talk like this to God, as to a friend.

I close these reflections by turning to the "Contemplation to Obtain Love" that Ignatius placed at the end of the *Spiritual Exercises* (230–7). His own experience brought him to see that God dwells in every creature, and that we can seek, find, and serve him as he labors in love to bring his creation to its final consummation. Ignatius invites us to remember with deep affection and gratitude all the blessings of creation and the particular blessing of one's own life, and to recognize that every good gift comes from God. One's life, one's own particular abilities and gifts are not just something that God has made or given. In some mysterious way, in creating us, God is sharing something of himself that makes each of us an image of God. One who recognizes that one's life, one's abilities, and gifts are a part of the larger creating and saving action of God, who is laboring for the flourishing of all his beloved creation, will ask God: How can my life and my action be more in tune with, and so contribute in some way to, what you are trying to accomplish? For as Ignatius well knew, real love—human and divine—always consists in mutual communication and sharing of gifts, and it expresses itself in deeds rather than in mere words. The desire to embrace and become fruitful in that love is what still inspires men and women today to pray Ignatius's *Suscipe*.

SUSCIPE

Take, Lord, and receive all my liberty,
my memory, my understanding and my entire will,
All I have and call my own.
You have given all to me.
To you, Lord, I return it.
Everything is yours; do with it what you will.
Give me only your love and your grace.
That is enough for me.

ALPHONSUS LIGUORI

(1696–1787)

August 1

Alphonsus Maria de Liguori was born in 1696 near Naples, Italy. His parents provided him with an exceptional education in philosophy, literature, and the arts. At sixteen, he was awarded doctorates of civil and canon law. At eighteen, like many nobles, he joined the Confraternity of Our Lady of Mercy hospital, devoting himself to works of mercy and compassion.

Following his father's will, he became a lawyer and was regarded as one of the most gifted lawyers in Naples. Because this work did not satisfy him at the deepest levels of his soul, he gave up law, entered the priesthood, and was ordained in 1726. Christ's claim on the heart of Alphonsus was absolute and irresistible. As a young priest he worked himself to the point of exhaustion. Caring for the poor was the hallmark of his calling.

In 1732, Alphonsus realized he could no longer be comfortable in his role of popular preacher, living apart from the poor. So, he left his family and dedicated himself to the service of the poor and most abandoned. He sought others who were called as he was, and adopted a style of ministry to preach the gospel of God's merciful love to the poor and most abandoned, especially in the form of a parish mission. And so began the Congregation of the Most Holy Redeemer, commonly known as the Redemptorists.

During a mission, a band of Redemptorist priests and brothers would come to an area to preach and conduct religious activities. They saturated the people with the sense of God. They lived in community in houses in the countryside so that the mission revivals could be repeated regularly.

Alphonsus was a brilliant, articulate, pragmatic preacher. He knew how to reach ordinary people who had limited education and very real needs. Three great images, basic to the Christian faith, formed the heart of his preaching and teaching—Jesus, an infant in the crib; Jesus crucified on the Cross; and Jesus vibrantly alive and filled with love for all in the Eucharist. To this he added the image of Mary, the Mother of the Redeemer.

Alphonsus wrote for the people and many turned to his spiritual writings. He emphasized practical approaches to reach those who were neglected or alienated from the Church. He also gave new life and direction to moral theology by preaching the redeeming love of God. The individual was called to love God out of an overwhelming sense of gratitude for what God had done in Christ. Not fear, but love was to characterize the Christian way of life. In the course of his long life, he authored more than one hundred books. Alphonsus would eventually be given the title "Doctor of Prayer."

Like many of his countrymen, Alphonsus was a man of passion and volatility. He found his balance and security in his devotion to the Blessed Mother. His appeals to Mary were impassioned, and he was confident that Mary would hear his prayers and that she was a great spiritual wellspring of his life.

Sickly for much of his life, Alphonsus' final years were marked by serious and debilitating physical ailments, especially arthritis, which caused him great pain and confined him to a wheelchair. He also was plagued with spiritual afflictions, scrupulously fearing he hadn't done enough to serve the God he loved so much. To help him through these times, his confreres gathered with him for prayer.

Alphonsus died at the age of 91, was canonized in 1839, and was declared a Doctor of the Church in 1871. He is recognized as a patron of confessors and moral theologians.

ALPHONSUS LIGUORI

Communicator, Counselor, and Companion

James A. Wallace, CSsR

It has been said that St. Alphonsus de Liguori was a convert, not to Christianity, but to Jesus Christ. After being raised in a Catholic household by a very strict father who was a commander in the Navy and a very religious mother, Alphonsus was given to scrupulosity. While he believed in God from childhood, in his early years, his was a severe God. Only gradually was his relationship with God transformed into a passionate love for the God revealed in Jesus Christ. The love of Christ, who was truly the center of his life, transformed him. This ongoing transformation led to his embracing three roles that continue to make Alphonsus relevant for our own day: an ardent communicator of the love of God revealed in Jesus Christ and expressed in the great mysteries of our faith; a wise guide and spiritual director whose counsel for living the Christian life continues through his writings on prayer, conscience formation, and the call to embrace the Christian moral life through practice of the virtues; and a friend of the poor and the most abandoned, who invites us to enter into the pain and suffering of our own world to bring the presence of our gracious and loving God to those most in need.

In the course of his life, Alphonsus was not only a great and tireless preacher to those most in need of hearing about the mercy of God, but also an author of 111 books and pamphlets, ranging from large tomes of moral theology to works for confessors and preachers, to meditations for deepening a love for and devotion to Jesus in the Blessed Sacrament and to his mother Mary. His desire to draw others into an understanding of, an appreciation for, and response to God's love embodied in Jesus became the foundation of his life and ministry. At the heart of his preaching and writing was his own great love for God, whom he came to know and proclaim as *iddio idiota*—"God crazy in love with us." This God was revealed to him in his experience of Jesus as redeemer and savior.

Alphonsus was dedicated to communicating the heart of God, God's great compassionate love for us, and his major goal was to draw all others to respond in a heartfelt manner. In an audience given in 2011, Pope Benedict XVI said that "Alphonsus' gentle and mild manner originated from his intense rapport with God's infinite goodness. He had a realistically optimistic view of the resources the Lord grants to every person, and gave importance to affections and sentiments of the heart as well as the mind, in loving God and others."[1]

Alphonsus' spirituality rested on the great mysteries of the incarnation, the passion and death of Jesus, the Eucharist, and a devotion to Mary, mother of the Lord. In a world that was infected with a heresy called Jansenism, which only emphasized the distance and aloofness of God from us due to our sinfulness and unworthiness, Alphonsus countered with endless proclamations of God's mercy and forgiveness, the willingness of God to cross the boundaries that separate us and draw us ever more deeply into divine love.

Taking into account the Second Vatican Council's affirmation of the Church as a pilgrim people,[2] Alphonsus makes a worthy companion on our pilgrimage as persons of faith through today's world. Theologian H. Richard Niebuhr describes pilgrims as "persons in motion, moving through territory not their own, seeking clarity or completion, a goal to which only the Spirit's compass points the way."[3] Alphonsus' writings in spirituality offer both the vision of wholeness and holiness to be found in Jesus and clear directives for cultivating certain habits of the heart—the virtues—and the practice of prayer as means of cooperating with God's grace.

When Pope Benedict declared a year of faith in 2013, he pointed to what he called the "spiritual desertification of the world," observing that for most people, the world was a spiritual desert because they found little evidence of God and of people who believed in God. He then called on believers as God's pilgrim people to be beacons of hope and to point the way to the promised land. Alphonsus' voice can be thought of as an able and supportive coach supporting our efforts to place our trust and hope in the Jesus Christ.

Alphonsus proves to be a most vocal apostle of hope, especially in his approach to the morality of a Christian. His writings on moral theology steered a middle ground on the formation of conscience, navigating a passage between what was considered in his day the more rigorist approach of the Dominicans and the more lax stance of the Jesuits. His views were accepted by the Holy See during his lifetime, and, little more than a century after his death, he was declared a doctor of the Church and patron saint of moral theologians and confessors.

The late Redemptorist moral theologian Bernard Häring wrote that while the legalists of his day overburdened Christians with many strictures and outdated laws, Alphonsus passionately defended the redeeming love of God, not creating a system of law that must be obeyed in servile anguish, but creating human beings out of his own love and freedom. Häring concludes: "Therefore, law and the threat of punishment cannot be foremost in God's plan. In God the Creator, love and freedom coincide. In God's plan of creation and salvation, the indivisible call to love and to freedom is to be cherished."[4]

In his many devotional and ascetical writings, Alphonsus provides the voices of many saints, offering a rich resource for meditation and prayer. In doing this he sets before his readers fellow pilgrims stretching back through the centuries, inviting us to join them in faith and companionship. One happy result is that we may become friends with Teresa of Avila, Francis de Sales, Vincent de Paul, and the many others whom we probably have never heard of but whose wisdom can inform and even transform our lives.

Alphonsus' writings on prayer and cultivating the virtues make him one of the most practical advisors among the saints. His instructions on prayer have proved helpful in our own day. Tom Groome, professor of religious education at Boston College, in his book, *What Makes Us Catholic? Eight Gifts for Life*,[5] writes how helpful Alphonsus' advice on prayer was for his own spirituality. After struggling for years with the Ignatian direction to pray at least an hour a day and to follow a fairly set pattern of prayer, he felt liberated by Alphonsus' advice to pray whenever you find it convenient and however you find most conducive.

While emphasizing the necessity of prayer for salvation ("If you pray, you will be saved"), Alphonsus, then, encourages people to pray in a way that engages the whole person: mind and heart, imagination and the will. His simple method includes reading, meditating, an emphasis on expressing one's affections for God and Jesus, and, finally, making resolutions for daily life. Yet, even here, his main stress is not on a system or pattern to follow but on prayer being a heartfelt conversation with God.

Alphonsus also offers instruction for cultivating various virtues that are gifts of the Spirit, thereby living in a conscious effort to practice and integrate such virtues as faith, hope, love of God, love of neighbor, poverty, purity of heart, obedience to God's will, humility, mortification, recollection and silence, and self-denial.

Alphonsus founded the Congregation of the Most Holy Redeemer with the express purpose of preaching Christ to the poor and most abandoned. Pope John Paul II called Alphonsus "a close friend of the people…who went in search of the most abandoned souls…a founder who wanted a group which would make a radical option in favor of the lowly…a bishop whose house was open to all…a writer who focused on what would be of benefit to the people."[6] Truly he found his life calling in working for those most neglected and forgotten.

When he was a diocesan priest, he was taken by friends for some well-deserved rest up into the hill country outside of the city of Naples. There he noticed, not only that the people were poorer than those in the worst slums of Naples, but also how "priest-poor" this area was, while, in contrast, Naples was flooded with priests. His heart went out to these poverty-stricken and religiously uneducated people, which resulted in responding wholeheartedly to what he saw as God's call to serve them. His future took the form of ministering to their spiritual needs by stirring up their faith through offering parish missions, events that featured preaching that called for deeper conversion, provided prayer services and instructions that aimed to set people back on the way of salvation.

In our world of ever increasing division between the wealthy and the poor, Alphonsus calls us not only to bring the good news of God's love for all, but also to embody the gospel by enacting our compassion and care for others, especially the most abandoned. His love for the poor is found echoed in the words and example of Pope Francis who asks not only that the church be for the poor, but that it be poor.

Recently in a discussion about the legacy of our founder, a fellow Redemptorist suggested reading *The Practice of the Love of Jesus Christ, Prayer: The Great Means of Salvation,* and *Visits to the Most Holy Sacrament and to the Most Holy Virgin*. These volumes can provide a rich treasure of theological and pastoral insights. So often these writings are overlooked, even within the Redemptorist community, but are definitely worth a read. Through these heartfelt writings, may you find yourself catching a glimpse of the heart of God and, in the process, enlarging your own heart.

ALPHONSUS' PRAYER FOR PERSEVERANCE IN PRAYER

O God of my heart,
I know that you always come
to help me when I pray to you.
But this is my fear:
I am afraid that I will forget to ask for your help
And through my own fault,
to have the immense sadness of losing your grace.
Through Jesus Christ's merits, give me the grace of prayer,
the abundant grace to always pray and to pray well.

O Mary, my Mother, give me, through the love
that you have for Jesus Christ, the favor that I ask of you:
to pray and to never stop praying until death. Amen.

NOTES

1. Quoted from the general audience given on March 30, 2011.

2. Austin Flannery, OP, *Vatican Council II: Constitutions, Decrees, Declarations*. Dogmatic Constitution on the Church (*Lumen gentium,*), #48; Pastoral Constitution on the Church in the Modern World, *Gaudium et spes*, #45, 57 (Northport: NY: Costello Publishing Co., 1996).

3. H. Richard Niebuhr, "Pioneers and Pilgrims," *Parabola* (IX:3; Fall 1984), 7.

4. Bernard Häring, CSsR, "Doctor of the Church" in *Liguorian* (August 1996), 15.

5. Thomas Groom, *What Makes Us Catholic? Eight Gifts for Life* (New York: Harper Collins, 2003), 296.

6. John Paul II, "Spiritus Domini," Apostolic Letter for the Bicentenary of the Death of St. Alphonsus De Liguori. Taken from *L'Osservatore Romano Weekly Edition*, in English, 17 August 1987, 4.

Mary of Nazareth

September 8

According to religious tradition, Mary was a Jewish woman of Nazareth in Galilee in the first century. Her many names and titles include Blessed Virgin Mary, Mother of God, Saint Mary in Western churches, *Theotokos* in Orthodox Christianity, and Maryam in Islam. Mary, mother of Jesus and wife of Joseph, is the greatest of all saints.

Mary was with Jesus when he performed his first miracle in Cana. She also was present at the crucifixion. At Pentecost, Mary, the Mother of the Church, became the mother of all the faithful. She provides guidance and inspiration to those who seek to abide by God's plan in obedience and truth. The month of May is dedicated to Mary, Mother of God.

MARY

Full of Grace, Full of Compassion

Margaret Eletta Guider, OSF

The past several years have seen a resurgence of interest in Mary that is driven by a variety of claims, quests, and contexts. This interest is highly complex, for it arises out of many different theological visions, spiritual orientations, sociopolitical locations, and cultural-familial realities. It reveals a religiously pluralistic landscape where diverse Marian icons and images, along with their accompanying narratives, provide access and insight into the *history and mystery* of Mary as well as the doctrines and devotions that shape and influence our contemporary understandings.

Within the Roman Catholic tradition, reflection on Mary as part of the communion of saints involves navigating one's way through the intersecting channels of theological investigation and popular piety. Theological efforts to mediate Church teachings on Mary, rather than contributing to an ongoing sense of wonder, relevance, intimacy, and identification, sometimes can result in the creation of distance, separation, disconnection, and radical differentiation between Mary and the rest of humanity. However, popular efforts to promote particular devotions to Mary, rather than enriching, strengthening, and uniting faith communities, can lead instead to misunderstanding, turmoil, and fragmentation between the faithful and Church authorities. Mindful of these realities and their implications for evangelization, ecumenism, and reconciliation, there is value to be found in the identification of Marian qualities that resonate with diverse constituencies in ways that are meaningful, dynamic, and cohesive.

Among the many qualities associated with Mary, five merit special attention because of their significance for understanding and interpreting Church teachings about Mary, as well as their importance for appreciating historical and contemporary Marian spiritualities. These qualities include: *freedom, agency, generativity, transcendence*, and *compassion*. Attending to these qualities enables us to grasp some of the ways in which Marian spirituality informs and influences Christian life and practice. In the process, individuals and communities can perceive the deep and powerful connections that exist between Mary and each one of us, not only in terms of our relationship with God, but also of our relationships with one another and indeed, with all of creation.

The first Marian quality is that of *freedom*—understood as freedom *from* evil and freedom *for* good. While this quality bears a direct connection to Mary's sinlessness and the focus that is frequently placed on her purity, it also is a quality that underscores what it means to share fully in the freedom of the daughters and sons of God (Gal 4:3–7). Every year, on December 8, at the beginning of the Advent season, the feast of the Immaculate Conception is celebrated throughout the world with great solemnity. Occurring so close to Christmas, it is often incorrectly understood to be a commemoration of Mary's virginal conception of Jesus by the power of the Holy Spirit, when in actuality, it is a theological affirmation of the Church's conviction about the God-given freedom that Mary possessed from the moment she was conceived by her parents, Anna and Joachim. Born free *of* original sin, Mary also was born free *in* original blessing. Predestined from the beginning of creation to be invited to cooperate with God in the unfolding mystery of the incarnation, Mary responded in total freedom to become the "God-bearer"—the *Theotokos,* the Mother of God. For centuries, the mystery of Mary Immaculate was a source of ongoing investigation and debate among those invested in defining the precise theological terms under which the immaculate conception occurred. As some theologians endeavored to safeguard the full humanity of Mary, others devoted themselves to defending the privileges associated with her unique *freedom from sin* and her singular *freedom for God*. With the 1854 proclamation of the dogma of the Immaculate Conception, the Marian "maximalists" may have held sway over the "minimalists," but the fact remains that throughout Church history until today, the proponents of both "ascending mariologies" and "descending mariologies" continue to mutually inform the distinctively different ways in which individuals and communities of faith look to Mary for inspiration, consolation, and protection.

In reflecting on the *freedom* of Mary, "full of grace," we are reminded of our own participation in the freedom and grace bestowed upon us in Christ through baptism. This freedom invites us, like Mary, to assume a posture of single-heartedness as we stand before God in the very "this-ness" of our own unique and irreplaceable creation in the divine image and likeness.

The second Marian quality is that of *agency*—understood as the capacity to act in time and in history, the ability to say *"yes"* to an unknown, uncertain, and unfolding future, the inner desire to cooperate with God and with others, and the inner awareness of one's own vocation to be and to become. Each year, the Church's celebration of the feast of the Annunciation serves as an opportunity to reflect on Mary's agency as expressed in her "yes" to God (Luke 1:26–39) and depicted in countless artistic portrayals of the event. This "yes" that echoes throughout Christian history serves as a prime example of Mary's total openness and availability to the divine invitation to participate intimately and actively in the loving and saving mission of God. Coupled with the mystery of the Annunciation is the mystery of Mary's perpetual virginity—*before*, *during*, and *after* the birth of Jesus—as dogmatically proclaimed by the Lateran Council of 649. This affirmation, while a scientific puzzlement biologically speaking, points to a more profound relational mystery of *virginal* agency and integrity that defies the laws and logic of nature.

Taken as a model for both the experience of espousal as well as radical discipleship, the narrative of Mary's dialogue with the Archangel Gabriel as presented in the Gospel of Luke (1:26–38) remains a constant point of reference for the Christian understanding of grace-filled action, vocational resolve, and prophetic obedience to the will of God. Mary's agency serves to remind each "bearer of the Word of God" of the "intact character" of everyone whose actions give voice and vision to the hope-filled belief that the "promises made to us by our God will be fulfilled" (Luke 1:45).

The third Marian quality is that of *generativity*—understood as receiving from the past; conceiving, creating, and nurturing in the present; and entrusting to the future that which one has received, conceived, created, and nurtured. On January 1, as much of the world ushers in the New Year, the Church's commemoration of the solemnity of Mary, the Mother of God, speaks to the belief that Mary is not only the mother of Jesus, the one who is truly human, but also the mother of Emmanuel, God-with-Us, the Second Person of the Holy Trinity, the only-begotten Son of God, who is truly divine. In 431, when the Council of Ephesus declared that Mary must be called the Mother of God, the mystery of her Divine Motherhood was affirmed.

However, another maternal mystery, not unrelated, also demanded the attention of theologians, believers, and artists. The mystery of Mary, Mother of the Church, an ancient title used by Ambrose of Milan and intuited in the narratives of the Wedding Feast at Cana (John 2:1–12), the Crucifixion at Calvary (John 19:25–27), and the Upper Room at Pentecost (Acts 1:14; 2:4), likewise speaks to the quality of generativity.

Conscious of the generativity associated with Mary, we are afforded an opportunity to reflect on the ways in which we, too, participate in God's mission through acts of generativity that contribute to the building up of the Reign of God as persons in relationship. Like Mary, we have received an inheritance of faith that has prepared us to welcome the Word that has taken root in us (James 1:21). Attentive to God's revelation through scripture, tradition, and experience, we are called to be agents of evangelization in this new historical moment. The generative challenge before us is dependent upon faith-based partnerships, hope-filled cooperation, and mutual affection animated by a mysticism of joy. It requires the sensitive and perceptive creativity of Mary and Elizabeth at the time of the Visitation. It demands the courage and critical consciousness of Mary and Joseph as they endeavored to make meaning of God's action in their lives; as they welcomed the birth of Jesus in a stable; as they attended to the words of shepherds and Magi, of prophets and seekers; as they fled into Egypt as refugees; as they returned to begin a new life in Nazareth; as they frantically searched the streets of Jerusalem for Jesus, and finding him in the temple amidst the teachers, drew strength from one another and from the God who brought them together in an unprecedented relationship of unimagined generativity. Following the example of Mary as she accompanied her Son and his followers, the challenge of generativity also demands the discovery of how to nurture others according to their needs and destinies that they may grow in self-awareness, confidence, and resiliency. Finally, it sets in motion an unwavering commitment to a future full of hope; a future that is built on memories, but also on dreams; and a future that takes seriously the mystery of the eternal infancy of God.

The fourth Marian quality is *transcendence*—understood as the power and grace to overcome the physical limitations associated with bodily finitude. In the case of the mystery of Mary's bodily assumption, the nature of her participation in God's mission extends from this life into eternal life, unbroken and uninterrupted. Throughout the centuries, Church leaders and theologians endeavored to understand and explain how it was that Mary passed from this life to the next. Theologically speaking, if the Mother of God was immaculate and preserved from original sin from the time of her conception, then through the power of God she would be preserved from death and bodily corruption until the time of her assumption—body and soul—into the glory of heaven, "joined to the source of Life."[1]

In 1950, when Pope Pius XII defined the dogma of the Assumption, the world was a mere five years away from the end of the most devastating and destructive war in world history. Amidst postwar reconstruction efforts, the memory of millions of deaths by gas chambers, hydrogen bombs, starvation, disease, and every form of violence, vengeance, and dehumanization proved to be a constant source of loss and grief. For those who survived the war years, the task of restoring and reconciling humanity in the aftermath of the worst of times was a daunting one. For Christians, choosing life demanded a renewed faith in Christ's victory over the powers of sin and death.

For Roman Catholics, then and now, reflection on the transcendence of Mary as associated with the mystery of the Assumption makes possible a more profound understanding of the mystery of every human person—the mystery of every person's "coming forth from God" and God's desire that every person "return." Sharing with Mary a connectedness to the Source of all Life affirms our own capacity for transcendence and union with the God who has called each of us by name.

The fifth and concluding Marian quality is *compassion*—understood as the capacity to empathize with the experience of another and to commit oneself to the interruption, alleviation, undoing, or consolation of another's anguish, suffering, pain, anxiety, marginalization, oppression, or diminishment. Since the recording of the earliest Marian apparitions and manifestations, there have been numerous accounts of miraculous occurrences and supernatural events associated with post-Assumption visions, voices, signs, and wonders attributed to Mary and to her intercessory power.

As virgin, mother, sister, disciple, companion, spouse, queen, mediatrix, and advocate, the many faces and numerous titles of Mary have been revealed through ages and across cultures. Marian prayers, litanies, rosaries, songs, feasts, pilgrimages, novenas, promises, festivals, dedications, artwork, enthronements, and namings account for many, but not all, of the devotions, patronages, and popular pieties associated with Mary. Moreover, worldwide, countless movements, sodalities, fraternities, societies, congregations, communities, parishes, shelters, hospitals, schools, human services, and diverse ministries of mercy and justice, explicitly identify with Mary in the exercise of compassion united with the heart of God.

Indeed, Mary, as the poet observes, "with her wild web and wondrous robe, mantles the guilty globe…stirring in our ears, speaking there of God's love, she is the live air of patience, penance and prayer: world-mothering air…."[2]

THE CANTICLE OF MARY

My soul magnifies the Lord
And my spirit rejoices in God my Savior;
Because he has regarded the lowliness of his handmaid;
For behold, henceforth all generations shall call me blessed;
Because he who is mighty has done great things for me,
and holy is his name;
And his mercy is from generation to generation
on those who fear him.
He has shown might with his arm,
He has scattered the proud in the conceit of their heart.
He has put down the mighty from their thrones,
and has exalted the lowly.
He has filled the hungry with good things,
and the rich he has sent away empty.
He has given help to Israel, his servant, mindful of his mercy
Even as he spoke to our fathers,
to Abraham and to his posterity forever.

NOTES

1. *Catechism of the Catholic Church*, 966. [Cf. Byzantine Liturgy, Feast of the Dormition, August 15.]

2. Adapted from Gerard Manley Hopkins (1844–1889), "The Blessed Virgin compared to the Air we breathe," *Poems*, 1918.

HILDEGARD OF BINGEN

(1098–1179)

September 17

Born in Germany in 1098, the tenth child in a wealthy family of the local nobility, Hildegard was "tithed" to religious life as a child. From at least the time she was fourteen, she lived as a recluse with Jutta of Sponheim, her mentor, enclosed in a cell attached to the Benedictine men's monastery at Disibodenberg. Under Jutta's tutelage, she learned to read Latin, chant the psalms, and, very likely, to employ the herbal and medicinal knowledge needed for life in a self-supporting agricultural community of the day. Beyond that early instruction, she was largely self-taught. But her mind and spirit, in spite of recurrent ill health, went far beyond what she absorbed from the books and people around her.

From an early age, she experienced visions—often prophetic, apocalyptic, and deeply creation-centered—that led her to view the universe as alive with God's presence and worthy of human care and study. As she approached middle age, the Voice of the

Living Light commanded her to write what she saw and heard in her visions. Ten years later she completed her first great theological work, *Scivias* (*Know the Ways*, 1151), which encompassed the whole of salvation history from creation to redemption. *The Book of Life's Merits* and *The Book of Divine Works* appeared in the following decades. She also wrote highly poetic liturgical songs (*Symphony of the Harmony of Celestial Revelations*) set to melodies of her own composition, studies of nature and medicine; a musical morality play, *The Order of the Virtues*, and over three hundred letters to popes, bishops, princes, the Emperor Frederick Barbarossa, and laypeople of all ranks. She preached publically and with episcopal approval, making four journeys, primarily along the Rhine and Main rivers, preaching to clergy, laity, and religious about the need for reform of clerical and monastic life.

After Jutta's death in 1136, Hildegard became the *magistra* (teacher; for all practical purposes, abbess) of the small women's community, continuing Jutta's spiritual and physical care of the nuns and people who had sought her aid. As the community grew and her fame increased, she was instructed in a vision to move them to their own monastery at Rupertsberg, which she accomplished only with great difficulty in face of the abbot's initial refusal to allow them to leave Disibodenberg (1150). She later founded a second monastery across the Rhine at Eibingen where she resided until her death in 1179.

Hildegard would have been remarkable in any age. Widely regarded as a saint soon after her death, her feast was celebrated in Germany at least from the late fifteenth century onward. She was formally canonized on May 10, 2012, by Pope Benedict XVI, who declared her a Doctor of the Church on October 7, 2012.

HILDEGARD OF BINGEN

Prophet and Visionary

Francine Cardman

There is no single image of Hildegard that conveys the fullness of who she was, but manuscript illuminations that depict her writing or perhaps sketching her visions as she dictates them to her secretary, with flames of divine inspiration touching her head, capture a central aspect of her identity as a visionary, theologian, and prophet.[1] A contemporary sculpture,[2] cast in rough bronze, stands outside the abbey church of St. Hildegard in Eibingen, the horizon opening behind it to the Rhine valley. Clad in a loose cloak and mantle, her hair windswept across her forehead, her eyes downcast or perhaps looking inward, Hildegard appears solidly grounded and at the same time about to stride off on one of her preaching tours. The verdant mountainside and fertile valley below are the earthy counterpart of the *viriditas*, greenness, that Hildegard saw as the life force of creation, its healing power revealed in her herb garden as well as in her visions of salvation and cosmic wholeness.

A woman of immense faith and great gifts, Hildegard was accomplished in science and medicine, music, poetry, and drama. She was a theologian and moralist, preacher and prophet, and a prolific writer of books and letters. The large body of work that has come down to us easily qualifies her as the best documented woman of the first 1200 years of the Church's history. The many facets of Hildegard's life, the depth of her faith, and the astonishing range of her abilities suggest the complexity of this twelfth-century holy woman. Her "rediscovery" in the later twentieth century vastly increased our scholarly knowledge of her work.[3] Translations of her writings and recordings of her music made her known to a large popular audience, giving rise to multiple new images of her. Feminists and non-feminists find their reflection in her, as do religious traditionalists and dissenters, reformists and reactionaries, earth mothers and mother superiors, even the German pontiff who recently declared her a Doctor of the Church (October 2012). Yet Hildegard exceeds and often subverts our imaginings of her. She resists being made into our image, whatever its contours. Instead, she insists that we confront complexity and contradiction—in herself, in our own lives, in the church. That may be Hildegard's greatest gift to us; the virtue we most need to cultivate in our time.

Hildegard teaches us to *live* complexity and contradiction simply by being a woman in the Church. Exceptional as she was, she embodied the contradictions of her time regarding gender and authority. She describes herself, not entirely accurately, as *indocta*, untaught or unschooled, and ascribes her sudden and complete understanding of the Scriptures to a fiery light from God that flowed from her head to her heart. When the voice of the Living Light commanded her in that vision to "say and write what you see and hear," she refused out of uncertainty and humility, falling ill until she accepted the divine commission and began to write. She insists that the visions she records so vividly and the interpretations she unfolds so painstakingly come from God's eternal counsels and wisdom; that they are not "the inventions of my heart" but "the secret mysteries of God I heard and received...in the heavenly places."[4] Yet she sought the approval of learned men, including Bernard of Clairvaux and Pope Eugene III, for the *Scivias* (*Know the Ways*), the first of three theological works based on the visions. Making no claim to authority of her own, she was enveloped with the authority of divine inspiration.

Illness augmented her authority. Hildegard was physically frail, subject to migraines that likely were the neurological origin of her visions and to mysterious bouts of illness that laid her low for long periods. One of her biographers reports that illnesses often occurred when she encountered opposition from authorities, or when she herself was slow to carry out a divine command because of her "womanly fear." She regarded illness as chastisement, but also believed that "Through illness I am made strong." And she was: she embarked on three of her four preaching tours while seriously ill, gaining strength as she journeyed.

Faithful to the Church and to her cloistered life, in her seventies she traveled extensively and preached prophetically on the failures of the Church's shepherds. In the cathedral of Trier on Pentecost, she gave a fiery sermon, warning that "the teachers and the prelates are asleep: they have abandoned justice," and foretelling the apocalyptic vengeance with which God would cleanse a "womanish time." In Cologne, she castigated the clergy for their luxury, laziness, lust, personal ambition, and lack of zeal for God's justice. In Mainz, she denounced priests who had fouled the Church, defiling the body and blood of Christ with their corrupt morals. She delivered this daring critique through the prophetic persona of Ecclesia (Church), a dazzlingly beautiful but sadly sullied woman, who had appeared to her in a vision as she lay sick.[5]

In the last years of her life, the Rupertsberg monastery was placed under interdict, the nuns prohibited from celebrating the sacraments and from singing the divine office, which they could only whisper tonelessly together, their music silenced. Conflict over the burial of a man, whom chancery officials mistakenly thought had died excommunicated, led to the interdict. Knowing that the man had been absolved before his death, Hildegard refused to comply with their order to remove his body from the monastery's cemetery. Consequently, she and her sisters were effectively excommunicated. They obeyed the interdict while Hildegard marshaled evidence and powerful supporters to refute the officials; the ban was lifted some months before her death.

Renowned during her lifetime for her visions and prophetic voice, her counsel and her healing powers, Hildegard was widely regarded as a saint after her death. Efforts to have her sanctity formally recognized through the newly organized Roman canonization process early in the thirteenth century failed, however, due to bureaucratic delays of nearly fifty years and probably also a dose of papal politics. When Pope Benedict XVI decided to declare Hildegard a Doctor of the Church, he first had to arrange for her formal canonization.

The complexity and coherence in these lived contradictions is mirrored in the corpus of Hildegard's writing and the multiple bodies of knowledge from which they stem. Integration of these disparate elements through her own intellectual and creative processes is the mark of her originality.

As a scientist and medical writer, Hildegard studied the intricacies of creation, from the starry universe, to the winds that move over the earth, to the simplest plants and herbs. Her detailed observations of the medicinal qualities of plants and other elements of the natural world enabled her to classify and apply appropriate remedies to commonly encountered diseases and injuries. Hildegard's medical writings on causes and cures paralleled her theological writings on the divine ways and works of God, creating an integral cosmology that joined heaven and earth, creation and salvation, moral and physical healing.

As a musician, poet, and composer, Hildegard wove the "symphony of the harmony of celestial revelations"[6] into the liturgical life of her sisters and now into our prayer as well. Her hymns, sequences, and antiphons praise Mary, the "greenest branch"; invoke the fire of the Holy Spirit; rejoice in Wisdom's divine embrace; and *laud Ecclesia*, who gathers her children into an eternal symphony, the communion of saints. *Hearing* Hildegard's theological vision through her music deepens the ways in which we receive her wisdom and teaching. Similarly, the artistry of the marvelous manuscript illuminations in several works, designed to accompany her written accounts, enables us to *see* what she saw and to share in her visual inspiration.

As a dramatist and moralist, Hildegard reveals a sterner aspect: fierce admonition and sharp denunciation, the prospect of judgment, the consequence of squandered freedom, the foulness of sin, and the fearsomeness of its punishment. Yet stronger forces in her theology move this harshness toward harmony and healing: the synergy of grace that powers virtue in the struggle against the Devil, the fire of love that suffuses the will, transforms the heart, and forges the way toward radiant light and lasting life. We see and hear this movement in *The Order of the Virtues*, an opera that is one of Hildegard's more surprising creations.

As a prophet and preacher, she brought the message of God's justice and encompassing love to those who asked for her counsel, and some who did not. Her major theological works speak with the authority and judgment of a prophet. Emboldened by the spirit of prophecy and empowered by the voice of the Living Light, Hildegard preached to prelates, parish clergy, religious women and men, and laity, chastising and imploring them to live with zeal for God's justice.

As a theologian, Hildegard melds her two ways of knowing—seeing and hearing—into a distinctive voice and vision. She apprehends the vastness of the macrocosm and its divine purposes as well as the particularities of the microcosm. In her theological writings, she especially focuses on the human microcosm that contains within itself, in each individual, the whole of creation. She traces the arc of salvation history within the human person, across the life of the church, and through the incarnation of Christ, who is Wisdom (*Sophia*) and Charity (*Caritas*). Just as there are causes and cures of medical conditions, there are causes and cures of the human condition. Hildegard's mission as a teacher and theologian is to instruct, to delight, and thereby, to *move*; to apply a divine and healing rhetoric to the wounds of humankind, to salve and to save.

What do we learn from the complexities and contradictions of Hildegard's visionary life and works? We learn that to speak boldly and critically in the power of the Spirit and the strength of love is to speak faithfully to and for the Church. We learn that it is the responsibility of this faithful love to demand pastoral accountability and zeal for God's justice from those who lead the Church.

We learn that there is a broader tradition of theology and practice than we perhaps imagined. We learn that it is possible for the Church to authorize a woman to preach and for clergy and laity alike to receive her message and amend their lives. We learn that it is possible, too, for a woman regarded as *indocta* to be a Doctor of the Church and to school us in God's wisdom and charity.

Hildegard's life, her writings, even her path to sainthood and recent recognition as a Doctor of the Church, teach us to see and to hold complexity and simplicity together. She reveals the ways we can find power in weakness, faithfulness in critique and resistance, integrity in multiplicity. She invites us to hear "the symphony of the harmony of celestial revelations" in this present life and to long for that perfect symphony of the blessed in which the faithful will rejoice together without ceasing.

PRAYER TO HILDEGARD[7]

Saint Hildegard, you were blessed
With gifts of vision, prophecy, and song.
You gazed into the depths of creation
And saw God's Holy Spirit at work there,
Animating, healing, and sanctifying all of life
With a burning Love and all-embracing Wisdom
Made manifest in the suffering and risen Christ.

Share with us your longing for a Church reformed,
Humble and reflecting God's mercy and justice.
Pray that we might be instruments of healing and
Reconciliation in a world wounded by selfishness and greed.
Open our hearts to hear the prophetic voices of the Spirit
Wherever they call to us in the symphony of creation.
And inspire us to join that symphony, as you did, with
Every tool of human art and wisdom as we express
Faithfully what we see and hear of God's love.

NOTES

1. Madeline Caviness suggests that Hildegard is sketching her visions here and is the designer of the illuminations in the *Scivias*: "Artist: To See, Hear, and Know All at Once," in *Voice of the Living Light: Hildegard of Bingen and Her World*, ed. Barbara Newman (Berkeley: University of California, 1998), 111–24, at 115.

2. The sculptor is Karlheinz Oswald, from Mainz. http://oswald-atelier.de/ (accessed August 15, 2013).

3. See the essays in *Voice of the Living Light*; also Barbara Newman's *Sister of Wisdom: St. Hildegard's Theology of the Feminine* (Berkeley: University of California, 1987).

4. *Scivias*, Declaration, trans. Mother Columba Hart and Jane Bishop (New York and Mahwah, NJ: Paulist, 1990), 59, 61.

5. Quotations are from *The Letters of Hildegard of Bingen*, trans. Joseph L. Baird and Radd K. Ehrman, 3 vols. (New York: Oxford University Press, 1994–2004), *Letters* 223r, 15, and 149r, respectively.

6. *Symphonia, A Critical Edition*, with intro., trans., and com. by Barbara Newman, 2nd ed. (Ithaca: Cornell University, 1989).

7. Prayer composed by Suzanne Beebe.

Francis of Assisi

(1182–1226)

October 4

Francesco di Bernardone was born in Assisi, Italy, in 1182. The son of a prosperous cloth merchant, he lived an early life of relative privilege, doted on by his mother and financed by his father both in aspirations to knighthood and in camaraderie with the young men of the town. Popular, courteous, and fun-loving, Francis was a leading light among his companions and joined Assisi's army in a 1201 war with Perugia. Taken prisoner by the Perugians at Collestrada, he was held captive for a year, and subsequently experienced illness and a deepening spiritual crisis that increasingly led him from revels and military ambition to solitude and a search for God. He abandoned merriment and fine garments; on a pilgrimage to Rome he even exchanged clothes with a beggar and joined those who sought alms outside St. Peter's.

Not long after, as he prayed before the painted crucifix in the crumbling chapel of San Damiano outside Assisi's walls, he heard the voice of Christ telling him, "Go, Francis, and repair my house, which, as you see, is falling into ruin." Taking the words literally, he sold cloth from his father's warehouse to finance a restoration of the chapel, incurring his father's wrath and initiating a final break with his family and previous way of life.

In February 1208 or 1209, while attending Mass, he understood the true nature of his vocation when he heard the Gospel passage in which Christ tells his disciples to take no money, travel bag, extra tunic, or sandals as they go about proclaiming God's kingdom. Dedicating himself radically to Lady Poverty, he began traveling throughout the region, preaching the gospel to rich and poor alike and attracting others to follow in living Christ's life intensely, whatever their state in life.

Although he did not set out to found a religious order, so many men joined his band of "lesser brothers" that he was prodded to write a rule for them and have it approved by the papacy. This launched the Order of Lesser Brothers, also known as the Order of Friars Minor. With Clare of Assisi, he founded the women's religious house of San Damiano, just outside Assisi. Francis also inspired thousands of laymen and women to pursue lives of poverty and service to their neighbors.

His identification with Christ became complete when he received the stigmata two years before his death in 1226. Though he was never ordained to the Catholic priesthood, Francis is one of the most venerated religious figures in history. He was canonized in 1228, only two years following his death. He is the patron saint of animals and the environment, and, with Catherine of Siena, is one of the two patron saints of Italy. He popularized the *creche*, or Christmas Nativity scene. It is customary for Catholic and Anglican churches to hold ceremonies blessing animals on his feast day, October 4.

FRANCIS OF ASSISI

A Holy Poet

James F. Puglisi, SA

Why would anyone in the twenty-first century be drawn to a medieval ascetic? Because Francis is recognized today, perhaps more than ever before, as holy, and also as a great poet—a poet who loved to sing. This is one of the reasons for a resurgence in turning to some of his writings and episodes from his life found in the Franciscan sources.

Many have been fascinated by the *joie de vivre* of Francis, man (and saint), and by his choice of poverty that was never separated from joy. In this respect, he was far away from the sad faces of the exalted traditional monastic spirituality. His figure today is sometimes fragile and at the same time vigorous—lively and current. Close to the passions and the great contemporary issues such as poverty, disease, war, the relationship with the "other," and with the environment, Francis is an exemplary and exceptional figure, totally Christian in the choice to live fully the gospel, but one who has never stopped being a human being—and, therefore, a true saint, a poet who loved to sing.

Francis embodies a perfect model of peace and dialogue: in the course of his life, on one side, he had to deal with Innocent III, known to history as one of the most autocratic popes, and on the other side with the Sultan Malik-al-Kamil, "chief of the Believers."

Innocent III received Francis in Rome, where Francis convinced him of the authenticity of the form of life he was proposing and obtained oral approval. In August 1219, in the wake of the Crusades, Francis arrived in the Holy Land and introduced himself to the Sultan. He was ready for martyrdom, but his words so moved Malik-al-Kamil that not only did he return unhindered, but he also obtained permission to preach in the lands of the Sultan. His encounter with the Sultan resulted in an incredible history of dialogue, mutual respect, and friendship.

In his vision of the universe as divine harmony, Francis spoke to creation, preaching to the birds and admonishing the wolf. How could he not call a Muslim "brother"? The Saracens for Francis were brothers and sisters in one human family, and Francis' brothers had to learn to live with each other to be able to proclaim the gospel. Islam in his eyes was not the evil empire, but part of the human family whom Francis wished to evangelize through humble example and peaceful words.

The truth of the gospel animated Francis in every aspect of his life. However, it took some time for him to realize that this was to be his mission. The famous encounter of the young, searching Francis with the crucifix of San Damiano challenged him to find a better way than the life of illusion that he was living. His many attempts to find happiness all ended in failure, defeat, and illness.

Today the way to the small church of San Damiano is easy and accessible, but in the thirteenth century, it was in a solitary place without roads leading to it and well outside the city walls. Francis was already in a state of disarray and confusion. In spite of the insistence of his prayer, he still could not understand God's design or plan for him. Nothing seemed to bring peace and fulfillment. It is from the depths of this despair that he cries out "Most sovereign and glorious God." This is the prayer pronounced by Francis in Italian dialect. One can imagine this poet gazing at the broken, crucified Christ and seeing the open eyes of Christ gaze back into his soul as he cries out "enlighten the darkness of my heart and give me the wisdom to see and the grace to fulfill your will." In this prayer for guidance, one can perceive the spirituality of Francis, which is still relevant for us today.

Today we are surrounded with many illusions called "virtual realities," which do not bring fulfillment and peace. What Francis says about spirituality today is that one needs to be centered in the right place. By recognizing that God is most high and glorious, he confirms a right relationship between creator and creature, while at the same time acknowledging that God is the giver of all grace. Only faith, hope, and perfect charity can illuminate the heart and lead to a new life, a new existence.

The basis of Francis' spirituality is the recognition of the goodness and graciousness of God, who is love. This, then, requires the conformity and imitation of this love in practice of our relationships with each other. Francis sought first to understand the depth of the love of a God who sent his Son to die out of love for us sinners. Then, moved by this compassion, he, like Jesus, embraced all with the same love as the Creator. This gives perfect joy.

This spiritual stance is what motivated Francis' missionary and evangelizing spirit. He taught his followers to be among the poor as the poor—not to come and go, but to live and share life with them. He instructed the brothers to avoid arguments and disputes and to preach the gospel with words only if it seemed fitting in God's eyes. In the common life, in living and sharing in simplicity, is to be found the heart of evangelization. This is the "martyrdom" he desired, namely to live the witness of love that is found in sharing and serving. Unfortunately, today many romanticize Francis, which takes the edge and the challenge out of what he saw as the way to conversion. We forget that his first call was to live a life of penance (repent and believe the good news), which then leads to a life of love and service in imitation of Christ. In his struggle to have his Rule of Life approved, the pope first said that the Rule was too difficult, too severe. Francis replied it is nothing other than the gospel of Jesus Christ! This is what inspired him to make the gospel more accessible to the common folk. He wanted to speak the gospel in the language of the people so that the people could understand the language of the gospel. In this way, he is a model for missionary activity, which requires the translation of the gospel into a language that communicates the core message of salvation.

Because of his stance, Francis is indeed received as an ecumenical and interreligious witness to the construction of peace and right relationships on the human level among all peoples. Driven by the desire to imitate the same love that Christ exhibited on the cross for the redemption of all of creation, Francis, the man, the poet, the saint is perceived as building bridges to right relationships. A "lesser brother" (*frate minore*) is one who seeks to open a space for the other, to embrace the other, and to love the other in such a way that the other recognizes his or her dignity as a creature of Love itself.

Francis sought to restore a new dignity to those who had lost their dignity. He sought to restore broken relationships as he did for those between the Bishop of Assisi and the civil authority, between the town of Gubbio and the wolf (a *legenda* that actually speaks about terrorism and how it is ended because fear gives way to trust), between the Sultan and those who would do violence. His was the way of the gospel, proclaiming peace and all good (*pax et bonum*) to all of creation because to live the gospel is to proclaim the peace of the kingdom but most especially to live in peace and to respect the dignity of all of creation. For these reasons, Francis of Assisi can be seen as a model both of ecumenical relations and dialogue, as well as interreligious dialogue, peacemaking, and conflict transformation.

His holiness is seen in the coherence of what he preached and how he lived. As man, a poet, a Christian, a saint, this medieval ascetic has much to teach the twenty-first century.

CANTICLE OF THE CREATURES[1]

Most High, all-powerful, good Lord,
Yours are the praises,
the glory, the honor,
and all blessing.

To You alone, Most High, do they belong,
and no [mortal] is worthy
to mention Your name.

Praised be You, my Lord, with all your creatures,
especially Sir Brother Sun,
Who is the day and through whom You give us light.

And he is beautiful and radiant with great splendor;
and bears a likeness of You, Most High One.

Praised be You, my Lord, through Sister Moon and the stars,
in heaven You formed them clear and precious and beautiful.

Praised be You, my Lord, through Brother Wind,
and through the air, cloudy and serene,
and every kind of weather
through which You give sustenance to Your creatures.

Praised be You, my Lord, through Sister Water,
which is very useful and humble and precious and chaste.

Praised be You, my Lord, through Brother Fire,
through whom You light the night
and he is beautiful and playful and robust and strong.

Praised be You, my Lord, through our Sister Mother Earth,
who sustains and governs us,
and who produces varied fruits with colored flowers and herbs.

Praised be You, my Lord,
through those who give pardon for Your love
and bear infirmity and tribulation.

Blessed are those who endure in peace
for by You, Most High, they shall be crowned.

Praised be You, my Lord, through our Sister Bodily Death,
from who no [one] living can escape.

Woe to those who die in mortal sin.
Blessed are those whom death will find in Your most holy will,
for the second death shall do them no harm.

Praise and bless my Lord and give Him thanks
and serve Him with great humility.

NOTE

1. *Francis and Clare: The Complete Works*, trans. and intro. by Regis J. Armstrong, OFM Cap, and Ignatius C. Brady, OFM (New York/Mahwah, NJ: Paulist Press, 1982), 38–39.

John Henry Cardinal Newman

(1801–1890)

October 9

John Henry Newman was born on Old Broad Street in London on February 21, 1801, the oldest of six children born to John Newman, a banker, and Jemima Fourdinier. He was baptized on April 9 of the same year in the Church of Saint Benet, which no longer exists in London. The family was financially comfortable and owned both a town house in London and a country house in Bloomsbury. Newman had a happy childhood. His parents were practicing Anglicans, and their love of concerts, dancing, and the theater suggests they were not evangelicals. John Henry, who knew his Bible, had his first conversion experience and entered the evangelical wing of the Anglican Church at the age of fifteen.

From 1816 to 1833, he remained an evangelical Anglican while he attended Oxford University. He graduated from Trinity College in 1821 and then continued his studies at Oriel College, first as a student and then as a fellow of Oriel beginning in 1823. His second conversion experience caused him to enter high church Anglicanism in 1833. He helped found the Oxford movement, publishing tracts and sermons on the need for the Anglican Church to recover its catholicity. Following his conversion to Roman Catholicism in 1845, he was ordained a Catholic priest on May 30, 1847, and joined the Oratorians a month later. Newman founded the Oratory in Birmingham and later, with Frederick Faber, the Brompton Oratory in London. Newman was the founding rector of University College, Dublin, where he served for four years. Pope Leo XIII made him a Cardinal Deacon in 1879. He died in Birmingham on August 11, 1890, and was beatified by Pope Benedict XVI on September 19, 2010.

JOHN HENRY CARDINAL NEWMAN

Heart Speaks to Heart

Paul Gerard Robichaud, CSP

> "God has created me to do some definite service; he has committed some work to me which he has not committed to another. I have my mission. I may never know it in this life, but I shall be told it in the next. Somehow I am necessary to his purposes, as necessary as an archangel is in his. I have a part in this great work. I am a link in a chain, a bond of connection between persons. God has not created me for nothing. I shall do good. I shall do his work; I shall be an angel of peace, a preacher of truth in my own place. Therefore, I shall trust him. My sickness or perplexity or sorrow may be necessary to some great end which is quite beyond us."
>
> **Blessed John Henry Cardinal Newman[1]**

John Henry Newman was by nature a shy and retiring man. He had gained a reputation for teaching in the classrooms of Oxford's Oriel College and for preaching from the pulpit at Saint Mary the Virgin, the university chapel. Despite his popularity and the interest people had in meeting him, Newman rarely enjoyed making small talk. At Oriel College, the rituals of high table and what followed after dinner over port and sherry in the faculty common room were fueled by the conversation of the fellows. At these events Newman would often sit in silence or slip away to his rooms to play the violin. If one had nothing of significance to say to him, he preferred the silence. For Newman, silence gave one's intellect and imagination full reign. John Henry believed in a deeper form of communication, one that happened, as he would say, "heart to heart."

Created a Cardinal Deacon by Pope Leo XIII in 1879, some thirty-five years after his conversion to Roman Catholicism, Newman placed on his coat of arms the phrase *cor ad cor loquitor*, or "heart speaks to heart." The words originated with Saint Francis de Sales (1567–1622), a French bishop and great spiritual writer of the seventeenth century whom Newman revered. Francis de Sales understood faith to be a marriage between the divine heart of God and the human heart of the believer. As de Sales wrote, "One's words must come from the heart as well as the mouth, for the mouth speaks to the ears but the heart speaks to the heart."[2] John Henry Newman chose "heart to heart" for it is through the heart that one soul speaks to another and God speaks intimately to us. As Pope Benedict said of Blessed John Henry, "He experienced holiness as the profound desire of the human heart to enter into intimate communion with the heart of God."[3]

John Henry Newman's heart spoke to other hearts in his own time. His conversion in 1845 from the Church of England to Roman Catholicism had a profound influence on the lives of many people. Here was the most articulate advocate for the catholicity of the Church of England, saying by his conversion that reunion with Rome was the answer. Some of the earliest members of the Paulist Fathers including Augustine Hewit, George Deshon, and Francis Baker, who had originally been Episcopalians, would cite Newman's conversion as having a significant influence over their decision to become Catholic.[4] One early Paulist, Robert Tillotson, was a personal convert of John Henry Newman. Newman's Oxford tracts, together with his conversion, would lead a group of highly educated American Episcopalians into the Catholic Church in mid-nineteenth century and some, as in the case of the early Paulists, into the Catholic priesthood as well.

Newman had been a conservative evangelical since the age of fifteen. He would later criticize this stage in his life, describing evangelicalism as religious individualism that ignored the Church's vital role in the transmission of truth. While at Oxford, Newman joined the high church movement within Anglicanism. High churchmen argued for the restoration of catholic traditions, which they believed had been abandoned by the evangelical leadership of the church. Newman joined a group of theologians that included Richard Hurrell Froude (1803–1836) and John Keble (1792–1866), and together they began to write small tracts or pamphlets to initiate a discussion within the Church of England over its lost catholic identity. They became known as the "Tractarians," and their theological viewpoint came to be known as "The Oxford Movement."[5]

The Tractarians did not think of themselves as advocates for reunification with Roman Catholicism. Like the Anglican evangelicals, they saw the Roman Church as having lost its way, and its grasp on the truth of the gospel. What they sought was a "*via media*" or a middle way; they believed that a restored catholicity within Anglicanism would represent a purified channel of tradition that flowed back to the early Church. Anglicanism would be one of three branches of the Church's tradition (Roman, Anglican, and Orthodox) and from their perspective, the one closest to the gospel. Their tracts were controversial and made Newman a recognized critic within the Anglican Church.

By 1839, Newman was a celebrity among undergraduates at Oxford. Students flocked to Saint Mary the Virgin to hear him preach. His preaching would also draw a number of the faculty, who sat quietly in the dark recesses of the back of the church—such was his influence on the campus. Evening services were packed when Newman would enter the sanctuary in cassock and surplice. When he arrived at a lectern set up facing the center aisle, he would kneel down in prayer, and the church would become silent with anticipation. John Henry would read the Scripture for the day, and then deliver his sermon. One student wrote, "Some men but very few, like Newman, have the power of using words like a musician uses his instrument, to draw forth sounds that seem beyond the reach of earthly music."[6]

Newman's preaching style was simple; he would read one sentence and then pause, and then another sentence and pause again. He made no attempt at rhetorical effect, and he used no gestures. Yet as he read the text of his sermon, to his audience of students, his words seemed personally directed at each of them. As one participant noted, "His whole soul was in every word he uttered."[7] Newman's influence soon carried beyond the confines of Oxford, and he acquired a reputation within the larger Church of England with the publication of his sermons, which seemed to fill a void in an age when Anglicans hungered for spiritual guidance.

In the summer of 1839, Newman had a revelation that would begin the process of doubt, a process that would eventually lead him into the Roman Catholic Church. He had been reading the history of the Council of Chalcedon, an ecumenical council held in 451. Twenty years earlier, the Council of Ephesus in 431 had declared that Mary was the "Mother of God." This was in opposition to the Monophysites who taught that Jesus had only one nature, a human nature; therefore, Mary should only be called the Mother of Jesus. Ephesus based part of its argument on the teaching of a theologian from Constantinople named Eutyches who taught that Christ had one nature, a fusion of the human and divine. It was convincing in 431, but by 451 Eutyches' theology appeared underdeveloped, and it was condemned at the Council of Chalcedon, which stated that Christ had not one but two natures: human and divine. Chalcedon's teaching came about through the intervention of Pope Leo the Great who insisted upon it. As the church fathers noted when they announced their decree, "Peter has spoken through the mouth of Leo." Chalcedon would lead to a schism in the fifth century between Rome, the Monophysites, and the Eutychians.[8]

As Newman read this history on the development of doctrine, he saw an analogy to his own time. He would later write in the *Apologia Pro Vita Sua* (1864), "the shadow of the fifth century hung over the sixteenth." "I saw my face in the mirror and I was a Monophysite."[9] Rome spoke with the power of pope, being forever a guardian of truth. The Eutychians, the extreme party, were the Protestants, and the Monophysites with their middle way was the Church of England. John Henry came to understand that a middle road is just as schismatic as an extreme position when it is separated from Rome, and he began to realize that he had been wrong. Rome made extravagant claims that, as an evangelical, Newman had once rejected: placing itself on the level of Christ, emphasizing the authority of the pope, praying before statues, and teaching that the bread and wine of the Eucharist was the real presence of God. But if the Catholic Church was in fact right and the agent of truth through the centuries, so were the Church's many claims.

Newman withdrew from Oxford in 1841 and went with a few followers to nearby Littlemore to create an Anglican monastery. Here he prayed for guidance and finally on October 9, 1845, he sought entrance into the Roman Catholic Church from Passionist Father Dominic Barberi. His conversion would cost him his friends and family and his position at Oxford. He had become a pariah within the Church of England. It was one thing to advocate for the return of catholic traditions and rituals within the Anglican Church, but it was quite another thing to become a Roman Catholic. Perhaps the hardest loss he faced was that of his friends, as Newman held friendship to be among his most important values. As Newman noted, the hostility once directed at him by evangelicals was now replaced by that of high church Anglicans who had been his old allies.[10]

In February 1846, Newman left Oxford and met with Bishop Nicholas Wiseman, a scholar and the President of Oscott College, where he had created a study center for converts from the Oxford Movement. Newman was for Wiseman a major prize. However, Newman decided to go on that summer to Rome to the College of the Propaganda. Here he examined several religious orders with the purpose of joining one, but none of these impressed him. He was shocked at what he called, "the poor state of philosophy and theology." What impressed him was the number of nationalities; some thirty-two languages were spoken.[11] At Christmas he visited the Oratory of Saint Philip Neri, and it would be here that Newman would find a home. He was ordained a priest on May 30, 1847, and joined the Oratorians one month later. Newman would found the London Oratory together with Frederick Faber, who would serve as its first superior, and later establish an Oratory at Edgbaston in south Birmingham.

At the request of the Irish Catholic bishops in 1854, Newman went to Dublin for four years as rector of the newly established Catholic University of Ireland, now University College, Dublin. During this time, he wrote and published *The Idea of a University*, which explained his philosophy of education. In 1859, he published his famous article in the *Rambler* on the need for an intelligent, well-instructed laity: "I want a laity, not arrogant, not rash in speech, not disputatious, but men who know their religion, who enter into it, who know just where they stand, who know what they hold and what they do not, who know their creed so well that they can give an account of it, who know so much of history that they can defend it."[12]

Pope Leo XIII created John Henry Cardinal Deacon of San Giorgio in Velabro on May 12, 1879, at the urging of the Duke of Norfolk and other English Catholics. John Henry accepted the gesture as a vindication of his work, but made two requests: that he not be consecrated a bishop and that he remain at the Oratory near Birmingham. In 1991, one hundred years after his death, John Henry Newman was declared "Venerable" by the Congregation for the Causes of the Saints. This title recognized Newman's life as one of heroic virtue. John Henry was beatified on September 19, 2010, by Pope Benedict XVI, and his cause awaits a second miracle that he might be declared a saint of the universal Church.

Paul Gerard Robichaud, CSP

Blessed John Henry Cardinal Newman was convert, scholar, and priest. His conversion would have a profound effect on many members of the Anglican Communion and here in the United States among American Episcopalians. His scholarly work, especially his writing on the development of doctrine, stands out in an age when Catholic theology was thin in content. As a priest, his devoted care for the people of Birmingham during the years that he spent at the Oratory, visiting the sick and the poor, comforting the bereaved, and caring for those in prison, made him a popular pastor. Yet of all of his achievements, his role at the university, first at Oxford and later at Dublin, and his essays on the importance of an educated laity, make it appropriate that hundreds of Catholic university centers are named for him. In all his efforts, and despite his shyness, his heart still reaches out to other hearts. He is a model and teacher, and from heaven, he calls us to seek the truth in all we do.

THE PRAYER OF CARDINAL NEWMAN

Dear Lord, help me to spread your fragrance wherever I go.
Flood my soul with your spirit and life.
Penetrate and possess my whole being so utterly
that all my life may only be a radiance of yours.
Shine through me, and be so in me
that every soul I come in contact with
may feel your presence in my soul.
Let them look up and see no longer me, but only you, O Lord!
Stay with me and then I will begin to shine as you do;
so to shine as to be a light to others.
The light, O Lord, will be all from you; none of it will be mine.
It will be you shining on others through me.
Let me thus praise you in the way you love best,
by shining on those around me.
Let me preach you without preaching,
not by words but by example,

by the catching force, the sympathetic influence of what I do, the evident fullness of the love my heart bears to you. Amen

NOTES

1. John Cardinal Newman, *Meditations and Devotions* (London: Longmans, Green and Co. 1911), 304.

2. Saint Francis de Sales, *Treatise on the Love of God* (Rockford, IL: Tan Publishers, 1997), 235.

3. Pope Benedict XVI, *Beatification Homily: John Henry Newman*, September 9, 2010.

4. Joseph McSorley, CSP, *Isaac Hecker and His Friends* (Mahwah, NJ: Paulist Press, 1972), 131–53, 225–73. Clarence Walworth, *The Oxford Movement in America* (New York: The Catholic Book Exchange, 1895).

5. Owen Chadwick, *The Mind of the Oxford Movement* (Stanford: Stanford Univ. Press, 1960); C. Brad Faught, *The Oxford Movement: A Thematic History of the Tractarians and Their Times* (Univ. Park: Penn State Univ. Press 2003).

6. Vincent Ferrer Blehl, *Pilgrim Journey: John Henry Newman 1801–1845* (Mahwah: Paulist Press, 2001), 234–35.

7. Ibid.

8. Jaroslav Pelican, *The Emergence of the Catholic Tradition (100–600)* (Chicago: Univ. of Chicago Press, 1972), 262–77.

9. John Henry Newman, *Apologia Pro Vita Sua* (New York: Norton, 1968), 96–97.

10. Blehl, 348–49.

11. Ian Kerr, *John Henry Newman: A Biography* (Oxford: Oxford Univ. Press, 1988), 327.

12. John Cardinal Newman, "On Consulting the Faithful on Matters of Doctrine," *The Rambler*, July 1859.

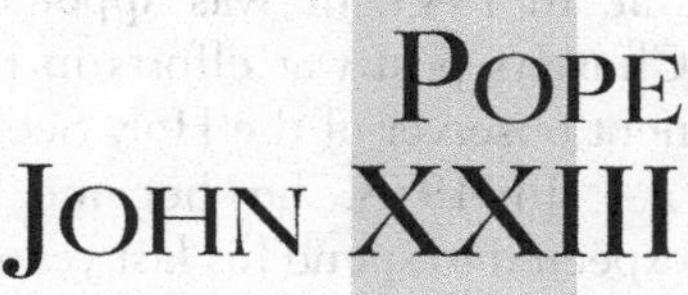

Pope John XXIII

(1881–1963)

October 11

Angelo Giuseppe Roncalli, the third of thirteen children, was born on November 25, 1881, at Sotto il Monte (Bergamo) to a family of sharecroppers. Young Angelo attended elementary school, and at the age of twelve, entered the seminary. A scholarship enabled him to go on to the Apollinaris in Rome, where he was ordained in 1904.

Continuing his studies in canon law, Angelo was appointed secretary to the new bishop of Bergamo, where he gained firsthand experience of the problems of the working class. With the entry of Italy into World War I in 1915, he was recalled to military service as a chaplain. On leaving the service, Angelo was appointed spiritual director of the seminary and opened a hostel for students in Bergamo.

In 1921, he was called to Rome to reorganize the Society for the Propagation of the Faith. Nominated titular archbishop of Areopolis, he immersed himself in the problems of the Eastern

Churches. Transferred in 1934 to Turkey and Greece as apostolic delegate, he set up an office in Istanbul for locating prisoners of war. In 1944, he was appointed nuncio to Paris to assist in the Church's post-war efforts in France and became the first permanent observer of the Holy See at UNESCO.

In 1953, he became cardinal-patriarch of Venice and expected to spend his last years there. He travelled to Rome to participate in the conclave to elect a new pope, and the Cardinals elected him and he took the name John XXIII.

One of his first acts was to enlarge the College of Cardinals with greater international representation. Less than three months after his election, he announced that he would hold a diocesan synod for Rome (1960), convoke an ecumenical council for the universal Church (1962), and revise the Code of Canon Law (1963). He wrote significant encyclicals: *Mater et Magistra* (1961) and *Pacem in Terris* (1963), advocating human freedom and dignity as the basis for world order and peace. *Il Papa* approved a new code of rubrics for the Breviary and Missal, made advances in ecumenical relations by creating a new Secretariat for Promoting Christian Unity, and appointed the first representative to the Assembly of the World Council of Churches held in New Delhi (1961). The International Balzan Foundation awarded him its Peace Prize in 1962.

Pope John died in 1963 and was buried beneath Saint Peter's Basilica. His cause for canonization was opened by Pope Paul VI, who declared him a Servant of God, and he was beatified by Pope John Paul II. Following his beatification, John's body was moved from its original place to the altar of Saint Jerome where it could be seen by the faithful. Bypassing the traditionally required second miracle, Pope Francis declared John XXIII a saint based on his merits of opening the Second Vatican Council. Saint John XXIII was canonized with John Paul II on April 27, 2014. John XXIII today is affectionately known as the "Good Pope" and in Italian, "*il Papa Buono*."

On his deathbed, John said: "It is not that the gospel has changed; it is that we have begun to understand it better. Those who have lived as long as I have...were enabled to compare different cultures and traditions, and know that the moment has come to discern the signs of the times, to seize the opportunity and to look far ahead." John XXIII's feast day is celebrated on October 11, the day of the first session of the Second Vatican Council.

POPE JOHN XXIII

"Il Papa Buono"

Diane Apostolos-Cappadona

> "Everyone remembers the image of Pope John's smiling face and two outstretched arms embracing the whole world."
>
> **John Paul II**

When I was a little girl, angels were intangible creatures, oftentimes looking like happy infants or ethereal adults. Always smiling, they floated above the earth singing God's praises. The saints were also found in icons and illustrations in Sunday school books. They were the heroes of Christianity who defended the faith, battled with evil, and lived in Heaven. But saints are not exclusive to historical times. Contemporary individuals could become saints through acts of moral courage to teach others the path to salvation.

Telling the stories of saints—like those of mythological or national heroes—creates an identity and a memory for a community by grounding us in the past while directing us toward the future. Religion scholars might argue that compassionate saints, such as the bodhisattvas, are made, after all, for the education and enlightenment of the living as well as successive generations. So we come to look to the future following the scriptural directive "do not be afraid."

POPE JOHN XXIII

Today, young people who grew up knowing Popes John Paul II and Benedict XVI often wonder what was so special about Pope John XXIII, so dear to Pope Francis I. Characterized by his humble and gentle nature, images of John XXIII abounded in the media and the popular press at the time. He was rotund with a warm smile, rosy cheeks, and twinkling eyes, welcoming all with open arms. Is this what makes John XXIII a modern saint? Is there more than meets the eye? What was he like? How was John XXIII, as he approached the dignified age of eighty, able to so astound the world, Catholic, non-Catholic, non-Christian, and even non-believers, with the courage of his convictions and his commitment to faith? How was John able to reenergize so vigorously both the Church itself and the public perceptions of Catholicism and spirituality?

The facts of John XXIII's life include his youthful enthusiasm for the religious life, his heroic endeavors on behalf of Balkan Jews during World War II, as well as his efforts at inter-Christian and Muslim-Christian dialogue beginning with his tenure as Papal Legate to Turkey and Greece. His own scholarly efforts at collecting, editing, and eventually publishing a multivolume work of the writings of Charles Borromeo by the much-respected Florentine firm, Olschki, which was not an ecclesiastical press, are less well known. Also less well known is the fact that he was a highly cultured individual, as evidenced by his statements and support of the arts and music. After a long career in the diplomatic service of the Church, John's fundamental desire was to become concerned with the daily duties of pastoral service, which he hoped his appointment as Patriarch of Venice (1952–1958) would allow him to fulfill.

Throughout his life, John valued the care of souls above any other occupation, so when he was elected pope on October 28, 1958, as a supposedly "transitional" figure, he sought to make the papacy more humane and the pope once again "the servant of the servants of God." John broke very quickly with the tradition of honoring an immediate predecessor in the selection of his papal name and began the demythologization of the papacy. Given his distaste for bureaucracy and the impersonal tenor of administration, John reestablished personal meetings with each Vatican department. Cognizant of the meaningful future of globalization for the life of the Church, he expanded the College of Cardinals by increasing its size and by making appointments of cardinals outside of Europe. Aware of the importance of the communication media as a mode of religious pedagogy and social entertainment for individuals and for the Church, he elevated the Pontifical Commission for Cinema, Radio, and Television to curial status.

John identified himself clearly as "the Bishop of Rome" and wore that mantle with authenticity by making his beloved pastoral duties a priority, beginning almost immediately after his election to make personal visits throughout his diocese. He first visited children infected with polio at the Bambino Gesù Hospital on Christmas Day, 1958, and later that same day spent time with patients at the Santo Spirito Hospital. On December 26, 1958, he initiated a series of regular pastoral visits with the inmates at Regina Coeli Prison.

A mere three months after his election to the Chair of Peter, John announced the three goals of his pontificate on January 25, 1959: to revive the diocesan synod in Rome, to invoke an ecumenical council, and to update the Code of Canon Law. Thus, he moved beyond the scriptural adage that "your young men shall see visions; your old men shall dream dreams" and put into action the dreams of his maturity with the vision of youth.

Formally, as the leader of the Roman Catholic Church, John XXIII refreshed both the individual faith of believers and the Church through his groundbreaking encyclicals, as well as his sermons and actions. He advocated human freedom and dignity as the basis for world order and peace. His life experiences and his faith informed his commitment to human dignity fused with humility, compassion interwoven with moral courage, and love infused with social justice. His encyclical letter, *Mater et Magistra*, issued on May 15, 1961, has been identified as a re-visioning of Christian teachings on modern social questions. In *Humanae Salutis*, issued on December 25, 1961, he called for an ecumenical council to meet in Rome and employed for the first time the biblical phrase that was to become the popular motto of his papacy: "to read the signs of the times."

When he opened the Second Vatican Council on October 11, 1962, John XXIII began his address with the phrase *Gaudet Mater Ecclesia* (Mother Church rejoices), unifying the interests of his papacy, his pastoral concerns, and his vision for the future of the world. *Gaudium et Spes* and *Nostra Aetate*, which reflect his concerns for interreligious dialogue and the renewal of the Church in contemporary culture, are significant documents issued by the council.

However, it may be for both his eighth encyclical *Pacem in Terris*, issued on April 11, 1963, while the Second Vatican Council was in session, and his "motto" that he is most remembered. John XXIII combined his commitment to civil and religious tolerance as central to the quest for universal peace to all believers. He also emphasized "the signs of the times" as crucial to three circumstances momentous for the future of the Church and of the world: the reformist expansion of the working classes, the increasing prominence of women in public life, and the elimination of colonialism. However, his pronouncements and his actions were always enveloped with his concern for the individual soul and with his compassionate love for humanity.

Historically, most saints were recognized for either the holiness of their lives or the sacrifices they made in defense of Christianity. However, contemporary saints may not be proclaimed through the manner of their deaths, but rather in the lives they lead, given the fundamental human weaknesses they overcame as they turned their frailties into strengths on their path to God. Their very humanness may be the essence of all saintliness. John XXIII's humility, his respect for the dignity of others, and his spiritual presence, revealed in both his individual character and the causes of his papacy, identified him as "good Pope John" to the world. Both the Christian collective and the world saw a reflection of the goodness of God in him; his ultimate accomplishment was his radically different and existential understanding of what it means to be a Christian.

As exemplified throughout John's life, the heart of the Christian message was Jesus' teaching of love. Whether characterized as *philia*, *caritas*, *agape*, or any other term, love was expressed through humility and compassion as the center of one's moral compass. Clearly many have written, commented, preached, and reflected on the significance of John XXIII, whose warmth and holiness caused him to be known as "good Pope John," but perhaps the editorial cartoon of June 4, 1963, depicting the whole earth shrouded in mourning with the singular description, "A Death in the Family," says it all.

The image of John XXIII with his two arms outstretched, eyes twinkling, and gentle smile exemplifies the warmth and accessibility of Papa Giovanni. Eager but nervous to meet the wife of the first Catholic President of the United States, the Pope practiced a myriad of greetings for "Madame Kennedy." However, when the doors to his office opened and she entered, John XXIII instinctively stretched out his arms and said "Jackie"—embracing her just as he embraced every individual and the whole world.

OPENING PRAYER AT THE SECOND VATICAN COUNCIL

We stand before you, Holy Spirit,
conscious of our sinfulness,
but aware that we gather in your name.
Come to us, remain with us,
and enlighten our hearts.
Give us light and strength
to know your will, to make it our own,
and to live it in our lives.
Guide us by your wisdom,
support us by your power,

for you are God, sharing the
glory of Father and Son.

You desire justice for all:
enable us to uphold the rights of others;
do not allow us to be misled by ignorance
or corrupted by fear or favor.
Unite us to yourself in the bond of love
and keep us faithful to all that is true.

As we gather in your name
may we temper justice with love,
so that all our decisions may be pleasing to you,
and earn the reward promised to good and faithful servants.
You live and reign with the Father and the Son,
with the Holy Spirit,
One God, forever and ever. Amen.

TERESA OF AVILA

(1515–1582)

October 15

Teresa de Cepeda y Ahumada was born in Avila, Spain, on March 28, 1515. She was educated in an Augustinian convent and entered the local Carmelite monastery of the Incarnation. Her convent years were punctuated by a severe illness. After years of meditation on Christ's agony in the garden, Teresa began to receive increasing mystical experiences. Through prayer and discernment, she founded a new house of Carmelites with stricter norms regarding prayer, fasting, silence, and enclosure.

Through papal intervention, she overcame the opposition of her immediate ecclesiastical superiors, and in 1562, she founded the monastery of Saint Joseph in Avila, the first community of *discalced* (shoeless) Carmelite nuns. She reemphasized prayer and poverty, using coarse rather than fine materials for clothing and wearing sandals instead of shoes. Teresa struggled to establish and broaden the movement of Discalced Carmelites.

In 1567, she was authorized to establish similar religious houses for men. Teresa organized the new branch of the old order with the aid of Saint John of the Cross, the Spanish mystic and Doctor of the Church. Although she was harassed by powerful church officials, she helped to establish sixteen more foundations for women and two for men. Two years before her death, the Discalced Carmelites received papal recognition as a province apart from *calced* (wearing shoes) Carmelites.

Teresa died on October 4, 1582, a gifted organizer endowed with common sense, tact intelligence, courage, and humor as well as being a mystic of extraordinary spiritual depth. She introduced a striking new model of religious life in Spain and powerfully influenced the reform of the Roman Catholic Church from within.

St. Teresa left to posterity many monasteries, which she continued founding up to her death. She also left a significant legacy of writings, including important works in Christian mysticism, such as her autobiography, *The Book of Her Life*, *The Way of Perfection*, and *The Interior Castle*, which used the metaphor of a many-roomed castle to describe the spiritual journey.

Teresa's writings, all published posthumously, are valued as unique contributions to mystical and devotional literature, as masterpieces of Spanish prose. Her poetry is often quoted and used in hymn text: *Let nothing upset you. Let nothing frighten you. All things pass; God remains. Patience wins all it seeks. Whoever has God lacks nothing. God is enough and all.*

Teresa died in 1582, was canonized in 1622, and proclaimed a Doctor of the Church in 1970, the first woman so named. She is the patron saint of Spain and of people in need of grace. Her feast day is October 15.

TERESA OF AVILA

Monastic Founder and Master of Prayer

Catherine M. Mooney

A sixteenth-century cloistered nun, devoted above all to prayer and contemplation, might seem like a pretty far-fetched model for most spiritual seekers today. Yet in both her deeds and her words, Teresa of Avila proves to be uncannily relevant to people living more than four centuries later.

The broad outline of Teresa's achievements is well known. When she was twenty-one, she entered a Carmelite monastery in her hometown of Avila, Spain. But her significant "conversion," as she calls it, only occurred years later when she was thirty-nine, an age then considered fairly advanced. Until then, she had struggled spiritually, rising and falling on a "tempestuous sea" as she puts it. Teresa's struggle and her belated awakening are encouraging: if it took almost two decades for a nun, one who would become a saint no less, to turn her life around, then ordinary seekers today can trust there is always time to strike out on excitingly new spiritual paths.

Like any genuine religious conversion, Teresa's carried with it concrete repercussions. She is best known for two achievements: first, as the founder of the Discalced Carmelite order, and second, as a mystic and master teacher of prayer. These accomplishments are reason enough to secure Teresa's place in the pantheon of

Christian saints. But can they speak directly to the concerns of busy people immersed in the events and responsibilities of this twenty-first-century world? Delving deeper into the lesser-known details of Teresa's life, exploring the complexities, even paradoxes, undergirding these "great deeds," we find someone surprisingly grounded in our human world.

Most people are unfamiliar about what Teresa had to achieve to establish the Discalced ("barefoot") Carmelites. After her conversion, Teresa was convinced that God wanted her to found a single monastic house within the order she had entered, the Order of Carmel. Teresa's project began small with just this one house. Under her leadership, it would crescendo into an entire movement that eventually gave birth to a new religious order of women and men, the Discalced Carmelites. Paradoxically, founding houses of contemplative prayer required her to spend much of her life outside the monastery walls. Against extreme odds, she had to be an astute politician, fend off an army of opponents, and negotiate (often surreptitiously) for the property she needed to make her new foundations.

Teresa's first foundation, the monastery of St. Joseph, is a dramatic case in point. Teresa tells the story in her autobiographical work, *The Book of Her Life*.[1] She spent her first twenty-seven years of religious life in the monastery of the Incarnation. While nuns from poor backgrounds barely got by, the well-born resided in relative luxury in monastic apartments outfitted with kitchens and often a cook and servants, too. Teresa, one of the privileged nuns, often left the Incarnation to visit friends, relatives, go on pilgrimage, console someone, or, when ill, be cared for by a relative. Her comings and goings broke no rules, but she came to think that a more strictly enclosed, poorer life would be better and, in prayer, became convinced this was also God's will for her. The diplomacy required to found a stricter monastery was daunting. She strategized, with mixed success, with a friendly widow about how to finance it. She next launched into complex, even byzantine negotiations to win approval for her plan. The list of male authorities she consulted is dizzying. They included her Jesuit spiritual confessor, her Carmelite provincial (a male superior always governed the women), a saintly Franciscan, a revered layman, two learned Dominicans, and others. The men didn't agree and some waffled between supporting and opposing her foundation. When word of Teresa's idea leaked, the other nuns in her monastery were up in arms, feeling their lifestyle unfairly criticized. Some wanted Teresa thrown into the monastic prison (yes, monasteries had prisons!). Throughout the city, Teresa became the subject of harsh gossip and ridicule. Many argued a poor monastery would drain city resources. Many religious authorities thought it would compete for alms given to their institutions. Others objected that the egalitarian structure Teresa proposed for St. Joseph's violated "proper" distinctions of social status and launched a lengthy lawsuit.

Teresa was savvy and worked the system throughout this period. She advanced the new foundation in secrecy, intentionally hiding information from her own Carmelite provincial. When her Jesuit confessor told her the project provoked scandal and she should quit talking about it, she complied, but only for six months. As soon as she saw an opening, she argued again in its favor and convinced both her confessor and his superior. After Teresa succeeded in opening St. Joseph's, she would go on to found—often after arduous fights—sixteen more monasteries for women and two for men. These would become the Order of Discalced Carmelites.

What's fascinating is that Teresa believed fervently in obedience and took great pains to justify her behavior in terms of that virtue. She could hide information from her Carmelite provincial by pointing to her obedience to other authorities, such as her confessor or a well-regarded theologian, when they agreed with her. Arguing her way through a thicket of hesitant and opposing authorities, she revealingly wrote: "If I found some person who would help me, I became very happy." Teresa told some who first favored her plan and then opposed it that their changeability justified her decision to stick with their first opinion.[2] One of her most strategic moves was to petition Rome directly for the approval she sought, effectively going over the heads of people who might otherwise resist. But Teresa's true trump card was heavenly authorization from the likes of St. Clare of Assisi, St. Joseph, Our Lady, and, of course, the Lord Himself. She said they unanimously wanted her to found St. Joseph's. Teresa wrote, "it distressed me not to give obedience to the [Carmelite] order, but the Lord had told me it wasn't suitable to give it to my superiors."[3] In short, Teresa always obeyed what she deemed to be higher authorities, be they human, saintly, or divine.

One might suspect that Teresa's visions and locutions conveniently justified what appear to be her all-too-human maneuvers. But this overlooks a central tenet of her spirituality: God is found within one's deepest self, not outside of us in some other world. She believed her plan was God's plan because her interior journey to self-knowledge, to God's very image within, put her in touch with God. Far from the shallow stereotype of an otherworldly nun, Teresa embraced what is human. Teresa exemplified the saying: "Pray as if everything depends on God, but work as if everything depends on you."[4]

Teresa was a mystic *par excellence*. The Renaissance artist Bernini famously depicted one of her many encounters with God in his masterful sculpture "Saint Teresa in Ecstasy." Today, exaggerated (and sometimes voyeuristic) attention to Teresa's mystic flights can create a false image of her as completely "otherworldly." It was her profound union with God, however, that kept her engaged with this world.

This is evident in her prolific writing. It was long thought that Teresa wrote only because she was following her confessors' orders. And while confessors did tell her to write many of her works, comprising five hefty volumes,[5] it is also evident that Teresa sometimes accentuated their orders because they gave her cover in an age when most people thought women should be silent. Teresa humbly *and* strategically acknowledged her lack of learning, but also continued to write because she knew her insights and advice could help others.

She treasured devotional books in her native Spanish. When, during her first twenty years as a nun, she could find no confessor who understood her, she relied instead on spiritual books. She was devastated in 1559 when, in a clear overreaction to the Protestant Reformation, the Inquisitor, Fernando Valdés, put most of the books she treasured on the first Index of Prohibited Books. Unable, like some, to read the Latin versions still permitted, Teresa took heart when she heard the Lord say to her: "Don't be sad, for I shall give you a living book"—by which he meant himself. But instead of passively savoring this private gift, Teresa, true to character, took public action too. It is no coincidence that she penned her first major work, her *Book*, in the years just following the Index. Her *Book* recounted all the favors God had shown her and included a long treatise on prayer. To her and her sisters' great chagrin, authorities never allowed her *Book* to be published during her lifetime. Some of her confessors and censors worried about sharing Teresa's personal account of her mystical life. Undeterred, when her sisters clamored to know what her *Book* had said about prayer, she wrote another Spanish treatise, *The Way of Perfection*, to help them and others.[6]

Despite both her protestations of inadequacy and her respect for learned confessors, Teresa was not above skewering them when they lacked spiritual experience. She criticized an unnamed confessor (probably one of her own), remarking that the Lord often "makes a little old woman" wiser that a "very learned man."[7] Teresa's chapter titles sometimes betray an amusing self-confidence in her ability to help others. She concluded one this way: "This should be read attentively, for the explanation is presented in a very subtle way and there are many noteworthy things."[8] Teresa was bold, paradoxically, because she was humble. It was because she attributed all her wisdom to God that she was convinced her words needed to be preserved in writing. She knew they would help more people after she died.

Teresa's most astounding engagement with this world appears, ironically, in her discussion of mystical flights *from* this world. She deeply appreciated the grace of mystical encounters with the divine, but refused to over-value them. "Sanctity," she taught, does not consist in "rapture, revelations, and visions" and people who receive such experiences are no holier than others.[9] Instead, Teresa uplifted human virtues everyone can cultivate, especially humility, detachment, and love of neighbor. Far from being the removed mystic, Teresa outlined the path to holiness open to all. "It's not necessary to go to heaven" to find God, she wrote, for God resides in the deepest center of each person.[10] Paradoxically, this interior journey to God entails also a journey outside of the self; hence her accent on humility, detachment, and love of others. "True perfection," she taught, "consists in love of God and neighbor."[11]

Teresa, ever the contemplative, was also ever the activist engaged with the world, making foundations, "playing politics" when necessary, teaching, and writing to help her contemporaries and countless generations thereafter. She reminded her sisters who might be saddened when called from solitude to work in the kitchen that "the Lord walks among the pots and pans."[12] For people today immersed in the busy details of family, friends, and work, Teresa suggests that all of life can be a prayer. As she put it, echoing Ignatius of Loyola, we can "find God in all things."

THIRST FOR SOULS[13]

Oh, my Jesus, how great is the love
You bear the children of the earth,
for the greatest service one can render You
is to leave You for their sake and their benefit—
and then You are possessed more completely.
For although the will isn't so satisfied
through enjoyment [of Your consolations],
the soul rejoices because it is pleasing You.

And it sees that while we live this mortal life,
earthly joys are uncertain,
even when they seem to be given by You,
if they are not accompanied by love of neighbor.
Whoever fails to love their neighbor,
fails to love You, my Lord,
since we see You showed the very great love
You have for the children of Adam by shedding so much blood.

NOTES

1. In *The Book of Her Life* (hereafter *Book*, cited by chapter, then section number), vol. 1, chap. 32–36, in *The Collected Works of St. Teresa of Avila*, 3 vols., trans. Kieran Kavanaugh and Otilio Rodriguez (Washington, DC: ICS Publications, 1976–85) (hereafter *Works*).

2. *Book* 35:4.

3. *Book* 33:16.

4. Often wrongly attributed to Ignatius of Loyola.

5. *The Collected Letters of St. Teresa of Avila*, 2 vols., trans. Kieran Kavanaugh (Washington, DC: ICS Publications, 2001–7); and see n. 1 for the other 3 vols.

6. In *Works*, vol. 2.

7. *Book* 34:11–12.

8. *Book* 18.

9. *The Book of Her Foundations* (hereafter *Foundations*) 4:8, in *Works*, vol. 3.

10. *Book* 40:6.

11. *The Interior Castle* I, 2:17, in *Works*, vol. 2.

12. *Foundations* 5:8.

13. *Soliloquies* 2, in *Works*, vol. 1. See also *Foundations* 6:15; and *Spiritual Testimonies* 40, in *Works*, vol. 1.

Isaac Jogues

(1607–1646)

October 19

Isaac Jogues, the fifth of nine children, was born in 1607 to a prosperous French family. He enrolled in a newly founded Jesuit school in Orleans at the age of ten and entered the novitiate of the Society of Jesus at seventeen. Following ordination in 1636, he felt a strong calling to missionary work and was sent to New France. Isaac began studying the Huron language with the noted Jean de Brebeuf, SJ. Brebeuf also instructed Jogues in the ways to conduct himself among the natives of these First Nations, learning to express genuine respect and sensitivity.

He fell victim to the constantly warring Hurons, Iroquois, Mohawks, and Algonquins in the area. Jogues and his companions were taken hostage by some Mohawks in 1642, who tortured and enslaved their captives. The Mohawks executed one captive for making the sign of the cross over a child. They severed Isaac's thumb and mutilated some fingers, requiring him to receive a special dispensation from Pope Urban VIII to celebrate the Mass.

Jogues eventually escaped with the help of some Dutch merchants and returned to France. He became a highly sought-after lecturer while he continued to heal from his wounds. With renewed energy, Jogues returned to the missions.

Serving as ambassador, Jogues tried to secure a truce between the Iroquois and the Mohawks. However, he learned that the purpose of the truce was not peace between the battling First Nations but to ensure that Christians would not be attacked. Jogues felt duped and returned to Montreal to resign. Soon after, there was an outbreak of disease and crops failed. The Iroquois determined that the black box with materials for the Mass left behind by Jogues contained a plague. On October 18, 1644, on his way back to the village, a young Mohawk killed Jogues with a tomahawk. Eventually this young man came to the Jesuits seeking baptism, taking "Isaac Jogues" as his Christian name.

Jogues' martyrdom was not achieved in a single act. Jogues and his companions endured torments of various kinds and were repeatedly tortured, beaten, and enslaved for several years. These physical miseries did not diminish their faith, nor deter them from their mission to bring the gospel to the inhabitants of these First Nations. Jogues and his companions "might be considered" a model for those who suffer.

Pope Pius XI canonized Isaac Jogues along with seven other North American martyrs on June 29, 1930.

ISAAC JOGUES

Missionary to North America

Paula Cuozzo

While others of his day looked to the Americas as a land of economic opportunity and gain, Isaac Jogues imagined these new lands as the fertile ground of evangelization. Captivated by the stories of Jesuit missionaries in North America, he too sought adventure and the occasion to serve God by bringing the gospel to these natives.

An able and recognized scholar and a cultured professor of literature at Rouen, France, Jogues chose to leave the comfortable amenities of his homeland and potential career promotion within the Church to face the dangers and privations of the New France wilderness and minister to the natives. Such personal sacrifice and willingness to follow the divine call sends a profound message to selfish and self-absorbed persons often found in our modern society.

One often considers martyrdom as a single event resulting in death. Yet martyrdom, as shown in the letters and journals of Isaac Jogues, can be endured through a continuum of events lasting for years. Jogues endured harsh weather, disease, extreme solitude, torture, enslavement, and, finally, a violent death by tomahawk. Experiencing the intense cold, traversing uncharted waters, undergoing long trips in thick forests, and lacking nutritious food and protective shelter did not daunt this New World religious pioneer's commitment and perseverance.

This saint grasped that entrusting one's life to God's will is not a singular moment of conversion; instead, faithfulness in vocation is an act of fortitude and resilience. Because Jogues and his companions were repeatedly tortured, beaten, and enslaved, they might well be considered a model for those who suffer chronic illnesses, have been tortured, have suffered disfigurement, or have undergone amputations. During his enslavement of more than a year, Jogues experienced continual decline of his health until he was able to escape, return to France, and recover. Thus, he might be also a model for older persons who experience decline in their later years and for anyone who deals with ongoing personal challenges. Jogues' continued perseverance amidst a variety of difficulties and challenges neither diminished his enthusiasm nor deterred him from his mission. He put his life in the hands of God and remained steadfastly committed to Christ, the Church, the mission, and the people whom he served, even though eventually this led to his martyrdom.

While imprisoned, he wrote:

> I become more and more resolved to dwell here as long as it shall please Our Lord, and not go away even though an opportunity should present itself. My presence consoles the French, the Hurons and the Algonquins. I have baptized more than sixty persons, several of whom have arrived in Heaven. That is my single consolation.[1]

Jogues' strategy incorporating himself and fellow missionaries into the natives' culture was forward-thinking and wise. Long before the development of formal cross-cultural programs, he realized the importance of both learning the language and interacting with the new culture. His relationships with the native tribes were built on respect and kindness for others. Today's multiethnic, multicultural world calls for new levels of understanding and engagement as practiced by Jogues.

Jogues' dedication to his missionary work was buoyed by his admiration for his novice director, Louis Lallemant, who was never permitted to follow his own desires to travel east to spread the gospel. In his well-known book, *Spiritual Doctrine*, Lallemant accentuated the presence of God within each human soul and in the events of daily life. Thus, when Jogues arrived in North America, he approached the natives with an initial respect. There was mutuality in his dealings with the members of the various tribes. Jogues immersed himself in the lives of these natives in such a way that he himself was transformed from a citizen of France to a citizen of the gospel in the world. While recuperating in France following his enslavement and torture, he rejected the honors that came to him from the French Jesuits and the courts. Jogues longed to return to doing God's will in his ministry of evangelization and catechesis, helping to build the Kingdom of God in North America. Through his newly forged friendships with the natives, he adopted New France as his home and returned there as soon as possible.

Although he was a victim of the perpetual conflict and ongoing turmoil of warring native Indian factions surrounding him, Jogues carried the cross of peace in the midst of strife. Undaunted by the natives' negative responses and even by their betrayals, he treated these natives with dignity, and he worked tirelessly to convert and reconcile all tribes.

When he realized that his life might soon be over, Jogues remained true to the commission from God, and wrote to a friend:

> My heart tells me that, if I am the one to be sent on this mission, I shall go, but I shall not return. But I would be happy if our Lord wished to complete the sacrifice where He began it. Farewell, dear Father. Pray that God unite me to Himself inseparably.[2]

Known for spending many long hours in prayer, Jogues' spiritual life was central to his teaching and example. Jogues had a special devotion to the Blessed Sacrament and even named the body of water that is today called Lake George, "Lake of the Blessed Sacrament."

Jogues also understood that to be an effective missionary, he must respect indigenous people and learn their ways when living among them. He became fluent in the languages of the Hurons, Iroquois, and Mohawks so he could gain their trust and bring them the gospel of Jesus Christ. He and his companions immersed themselves in the local culture and treated these natives with dignity. Jogues also taught them European techniques for cultivating crops and raising livestock. Isaac Jogues is a saint who had sensitivity to inculturation and fervor for evangelizing the First Nations in the lands that would become parts of Canada and the United States.

Evangelizer to the Native Americans, Jogues was a role model for reconciliation and embraced an ecumenical approach four hundred years ago that remains relevant today. The Mohawks rightly called Jogues "the indomitable one."

PRAYER FOR NORTH AMERICAN MISSIONARIES[3]

Loving God, you called Isaac Jogues and his companions
to be caring and courageous missionaries
to preach the gospel in North America.
St. Isaac dedicated his life to sharing his love for you
by spreading the good news of God's love to all peoples.
May the missionary blood shed for Christ inspire us
with zeal in our evangelization.
Remembering the spirit of Issac Jogues,
may we grow in compassion and courage
to be strong and gentle messengers of your love.
Through intercession of the Isaac Jogues,
draw your children closer to Jesus Christ, who lives

and reigns with you and the Holy Spirit, one God,
forever and ever. Amen.

NOTES

1. Francis X. Talbot, SJ, *Saint Among Savages: The Life of St. Isaac Jogues* (New York: Harper and Brothers, 1935. Reprint, San Francisco: Ignatius Press, 2002), 297.

2. Vincent J. O'Malley, *Saints of North America* (Huntington, IN: Our Sunday Visitor Publishing, 2004), 414.

3. Prayer composed by Paula Cuozzo and Thomas A. Kane, CSP.

Dorothy Day

(1897–1980)

November 29

Dorothy Day was born in 1897 in New York City. She started out as a journalist, writing for several socialist and progressive publications in the 1910s and 1920s. Intrigued by the Catholic faith for years, she converted. In 1933, Day worked closely with fellow activist Peter Maurin to establish the Catholic Worker, a nonviolent, pacifist movement that continues today to combine direct aid for the poor and homeless with nonviolent direct action on their behalf. As part of the movement's belief in hospitality, Day helped establish special homes for those in need.

Dorothy Day dedicated much of her life in service to her socialist beliefs and her adopted faith, Catholicism. She died at Maryhouse, one of the Catholic settlement houses she helped establish. Almost immediately after her death in 1980, controversy arose about whether she should be canonized a saint by the Church. Now that the Vatican has approved the late Cardinal John O'Connor's request to consider Dorothy Day's "cause," the controversy is being rekindled. Voices opposing the process say that Dorothy Day shunned the suggestion she was a saint, and they believe she would rather have any money spent on her canonization given to the poor. Others are concerned that her radical vision will be sanitized and spun to support Catholic traditionalism, neutralizing her ardent pacifism, radical critique of society, and love of the poor. Many voices are in support of the canonization process, citing Dorothy Day's life as an example that has inspired them to prayer and social justice. Her faithfulness to the gospel, living the "preferential option for the poor" and showing that a layperson can achieve heroic virtue, are often cited.

DOROTHY DAY

The Seeker Saint

Brett C. Hoover

Dorothy Day is at once the most accessible and inaccessible of our modern holy women. Much of her spiritual journey feels contemporary, a search for spirituality familiar to many young people today. Sociologists call the pattern *seeking spirituality*. Robert Wuthnow describes it: "Individuals search for sacred moments that reinforce their conviction that the divine exists, but these moments are fleeting."[1] Theologians associate this restless searching with St. Augustine in his *Confessions*, "For Thou hast made us for Thyself, and our hearts are restless until they rest in Thee."[2] But many of our students associate the search not with Christianity at all but often with Asian religions like Buddhism or Hinduism. Curiously then, in Hindu tradition, seeking spirituality is the way of the old, of the *sannyasin* who, having completed family and economic commitments, devotes his or her life to finding divinity and escaping the cycle of rebirth. In that same tradition, the young choose what sociologists would call a *dwelling spirituality*, an attachment to the sacred as manifest in particular places and in the practices and structures of a settled life.[3] In our age, the timing is reversed. The extension of adolescence through education and delayed marriage turns *emerging adulthood* into an unsettled time of seeking and searching. Dwelling is relegated to the more geographically settled life of middle age. But perhaps because of individualism, increasingly, dwelling spirituality remains unrecognizable to contemporary people. Many students, young or old, cannot really conceive of a communitarian, settled religious faith. For better or for worse, faith to them is always about an individual's restless search for the sacred.

Wuthnow sees seeking spirituality as particularly suited to unstable, changing times, and both Dorothy Day and our postmodern young people have lived in such times. Raised with only a modicum of religion, Day came of age in Jazz Age New York City, writing and editing for socialist newspapers, participating in radical politics, and wandering through a string of love affairs. She could not avoid a recurring attraction to spiritual questions, but she rejected religion outright. "In my youthful arrogance, in my feeling that I was one of the strong, I felt then for the first time that religion was something I must ruthlessly cut out of my life."[4] Today's young people do not necessarily think of religion as for the weak (except perhaps some of the more scientifically bent); but they do associate it more or less exclusively with that brand of contemporary social conservatism that has congealed around opposition to gay marriage. Some find this congenial, but most do not.

Day's own restless searching brought her back again and again to Roman Catholicism. Young people today may find comfort in the ambivalence she felt. She loved Catholicism for being the religion of the poor, though she knew it often catered to the rich. "I was just as much against capitalism and imperialism as ever, and here I was going over to the opposition, because, of course, the Church was lined up with property, with the wealth, with the state, with capitalism, with all the forces of reaction."[5] For many months, she remained in an in-between space, desperately wanting the Catholic faith but unable to swallow its association with what she considered retrogressive politics. But her daughter Tamar's birth precipitated a spiritual crisis, and after she met a Sister of Charity on the street, she became determined to see Tamar baptized as a Catholic. Gradually that led to a parting of the ways with her atheist, common-law husband, Forster Batterham, and it led to her own baptism later that year. But it was not until five years after that she resolved the tension between Catholicism and her radical politics. The editor of the Catholic weekly *Commonweal* sent the itinerant French philosopher Peter Maurin to see her. Maurin schooled her in a personalist philosophy that accentuated the dignity of the worker, and he taught her about the emphasis on workers' rights and human dignity in Catholic social teaching. In 1933, they founded the Catholic Worker movement. The rest, we might say, is history.

Day's restless searching and struggles over politics have endeared her to the disciples of Isaac Thomas Hecker. Hecker also began in politics, seeking a more just order through a New York City political party advocating for workers' rights. He also underwent a restless spiritual search. Amidst the Romanticism of the mid-nineteenth century and the religious landscape of the Second Great Awakening, he wandered from Transcendentalism to Roman Catholicism. Day's own spiritual director for many years was a disciple of Isaac Hecker, Paulist Father Joseph McSorley, who authored the popular *Isaac Hecker and His Friends*.[6] Day reportedly became disaffected with the Paulists later on, because they had become "too comfortable." Even so, the Paulists continued to be some of the most articulate spokespersons for the notion of the spiritual life that Day and Hecker shared—essentially that everyone, given the chance, would undertake a spiritual search and find the extravagant God of Love.

Despite the familiarity of this restless spiritual searching to most people today (and perhaps the familiarity of finding God in Catholic community for others of us), Dorothy Day's spiritual search skews very radical for our middle-class world. The progress of industrial capitalism and globalization in our time would have horrified her. Day did not simply believe Catholics should care for the poor; she thought they should live with them—and she did, all her life. She believed absolutely in nonviolence; the Catholic Worker movement split apart when she declared her pacifism during World War II. All her life she remained a personalist *and* an anarchist. She saw the interconnectedness and inherent dignity of human beings as placing a heavy burden of responsibility on all of us in a world of squalor and inequality. But she also resolutely believed that only small groups and individuals could promote that responsibility. "Put simply, God wished us to be our brother's keeper."[7] She did not think that the government could do much, and she opposed extending tax-exempt status to charitable works and institutions.[8] She did not like the idea of voting in elections or paying taxes that supported the war machine.[9] She was vociferously an anarchist in an era when it could get one jailed, deported, or killed.

But perhaps today, even more than her radicalism, Dorothy Day's wholehearted embrace of preconciliar Roman Catholicism seems odd. She famously told Robert Coles:

> I was a Catholic then, and I am now, and I hope and pray I die one. I have not wanted to challenge the church, not on any of its doctrinal positions. I try to be loyal to the church—to its teachings, its ideals.[10]

In spite of her radicalism, Dorothy Day did not just assent to Catholic beliefs. She was in love with the Church. "I loved the Church for Christ made visible." She loved the sacraments and the identification with the poor. "I loved, in other words, and like all women in love, I wanted to be united to my love. Why should not Forster be jealous?"[11] This kind of love for the Church may seem more off-putting than any other part of Dorothy Day's journey. To understand, we really have to have Day's complex feel for what love is. Yes, it was extravagant and romantic, but it was also dogged in the face of the struggles and contradictions of life, "a harsh and dreadful thing," she would tell new recruits, quoting Dostoevsky.[12] Her love for the Church did not make her shrink from its hypocrisies and contradictions. "Romano Guardini said that the Church is the Cross on which Christ was crucified; one could not separate Christ from his Cross, and one must live in a state of permanent dissatisfaction with the Church."[13] Her love for the Church did not deter her from picketing Cardinal Spellman's office in 1949 to protest against seminarians serving as replacement workers for striking gravediggers. When Spellman ordered the *Catholic Worker* to cease publishing or change its name two years later, she (probably disingenuously) noted that her associate editors had outvoted her and decided to resist. Spellman backed down.[14]

Hearing stories like this, we might be tempted to accuse Dorothy Day of hypocrisy or (worse to her) playing politics. But maybe the seeming contradictions of her life—earnest seeker, radical activist, loyal Catholic—provide us with what makes her most accessible to us. She was unwaveringly real. Her solidarity with other human beings dictated nearly everything she did. Good personalist that she was, she celebrated human life with all its craziness. She knew that people never escaped their loneliness, but she wanted us to care for one another anyway. She railed against excessive spending on grand churches, but she believed that the poor could find quiet and dignity in them. She never ceased to believe in the power of beauty, which she saw as transformative in a world of desperation. Once she gave a donated diamond ring to an elderly woman who came to the Catholic Worker house for meals. When others complained, Dorothy retorted, "Do you suppose God created diamonds only for the rich?"[15] She embodied the best of that Catholic personalism that has so captured the imagination of figures as diverse as Mother Theresa of Calcutta, Pope John Paul II, and Jacques Maritain. In a world eager to undervalue human beings for countless reasons—because they are poor or old or immigrants or not conventionally beautiful or in any way different—Dorothy Day stands as a witness to us, reminding us that it is not enough to simply search for God in our own hearts. We must find God in other human beings, or we are not Christians at all.

PRAYER FOR THE INTERCESSION OF SERVANT OF GOD DOROTHY DAY

God our Creator,
your servant Dorothy Day exemplified the
Catholic faith by her conversion,
life of prayer and voluntary poverty,
works of mercy, and
witness to the justice and peace
of the Gospel.

May her life inspire people
to turn to Christ as their Savior and guide,
to see his face in the world's poor and
to raise their voices for the justice
of God's kingdom.
We pray that you grant the favors we ask
through her intercession so that her goodness
and holiness may be more widely recognized
and one day the Church may
proclaim her Saint.
We ask this through Christ our Lord. Amen.[16]

NOTES

1. Robert Wuthnow, *After Heaven: Spirituality in America Since the 1950s* (Berkeley: University of California Press, 1998), 4.
2. Augustine of Hippo, *Confessions*, trans. F. J. Sheed (Indianapolis: Hackett, 2006), 3.
3. Wuthnow, *After Heaven*, 3–4.
4. Dorothy Day, *The Long Loneliness: The Autobiography of Dorothy Day* (New York: HarperOne, 1952), 43.
5. Ibid., 149.
6. (New York: Paulist Press, 1972).

7. Robert Ellsberg, *Dorothy Day: Selected Writings* (Maryknoll, NY: Orbis, 1983), xxviii.

8. Fred Boehrer, "Diversity, Plurality and Ambiguity: Anarchism in the Catholic Worker Movement," in *Dorothy Day and the Catholic Worker Movement: Centenary Essays*, ed. Phillip M. Runkel and Susan Mountin (Milwaukee: Marquette University Press, 2005), 98.

9. Patrick G. Coy, "Beyond the Ballot Box: The Catholic Worker Movement and Nonviolent Direct Action," in *Dorothy Day and the Catholic Worker Movement: Centenary Essays*, 171. See also Mark S. Massa, *Catholics and American Culture: Fulton Sheen, Dorothy Day, and the Notre Dame Football Team* (New York: Crossroad, 1999), 120.

10. Robert Coles, *Dorothy Day: A Radical Devotion* (New York: Da Capo Press, 1987), 82.

11. Day, *The Long Loneliness*, 149.

12. Massa, *Catholics and American Culture*, 107.

13. Day, *The Long Loneliness*, 150.

14. Brian Terrell, "Dorothy Day, Rebel Catholic: Living in a Permanent State of Dissatisfaction with the Church," in *Dorothy Day and the Catholic Worker Movement: Centenary Essays*, 146–47.

15. Ellsberg, *Dorothy Day*, xlii–xliii.

16. Composed by Monsignor Kevin Sullivan, Executive Director of The Catholic Charities of the Archdiocese of New York.

7. Robert Ellsberg, *Dorothy Day: Selected Writings* (Maryknoll, NY: Orbis, 1983), xxviii.

8. Fred Boehrer, "Diversity, Plurality and Ambiguity: Anarchism in the Catholic Worker Movement," in *Dorothy Day and the Catholic Worker Movement: Centenary Essays*, ed. Phillip M. Runkel and Susan Mountin (Milwaukee: Marquette University Press, 2001), 98.

9. Patrick G. Coy, "Beyond the Ballot Box: The Catholic Worker Movement and Nonviolent Direct Action," in *Dorothy Day and the Catholic Worker Movement: Centenary Essays*, 171. See also Mark S. Massa, *Catholics and American Culture: Fulton Sheen, Dorothy Day, and the Notre Dame Football Team* (New York: Crossroad, 1999), 120.

10. Robert Coles, *Dorothy Day: A Radical Devotion* (New York: Da Capo Press, 1987), 82.

11. Day, *The Long Loneliness*, 149.

12. Massa, *Catholics and American Culture*, 107.

13. Day, *The Long Loneliness*, 150.

14. Brian Terrell, "Dorothy Day, Rebel Catholic: Living in a Permanent State of Dissatisfaction with the Church," in *Dorothy Day and the Catholic Worker Movement: Centenary Essays*, 146–47.

15. Ellsberg, *Dorothy Day*, xli–xliii.

16. Composed by Monsignor Kevin Sullivan, Executive Director of The Catholic Charities of the Archdiocese of New York.

The Virgin of Guadalupe

December 12

It was 1649 in colonial Mexico. Laso de la Vega, a priest at the chapel of The Virgin of Guadalupe in Tepeyac, near Mexico City, published a book written in Nahuatl, the language of the Aztecs and their neighbors. His book told the story of a poor Indian convert named Juan Diego, who, in December of 1531, only ten years after the Spanish conquest of Mexico, encountered the Blessed Virgin at Tepeyac four times within four days. The Virgin asked him to go to the bishop of Mexico to request a shrine in her honor at Tepeyac. The Virgin told Juan Diego to pick miraculous flowers there and bring them to the bishop as proof of veracity. When Juan Diego opened his coarsely woven cloak to let the flowers tumble out, he found that the Virgin had imprinted her image on the cloak. This image was remarkable in its depiction of her as dark-skinned, like the native peoples of Mexico, pregnant, dressed in royal Aztec garb, and standing on the moon with sun rays shining behind her.

This account, known as the *Nican Mopohua*, was marked by

extraordinary beauty of language and the tenderness of exchanges between Juan Diego and the Virgin. It became the standard origin account of The Virgin of Guadalupe in Mexico, following the first Spanish account by only a year.

No written testimony concerning Juan Diego and his visions had existed before 1648, and documentation of any kind was, and still is, meager at best. But devotion to Guadalupe has grown without it and continues to grow through almost five hundred years, first in the Americas and now beyond. The basic message spoken to Juan Diego and captured in the image on his cloak was powerful: we are all, even the conquered, downtrodden, powerless, and despised, equally loved by God, and Mary is the loving mother of all in her motherhood of God's Son. Mary continues to do the work of her Son in drawing people to God through the ages.

THE VIRGIN OF GUADALUPE

"Dar a Luz" (Apparition 1531)

Nancy Pineda-Madrid

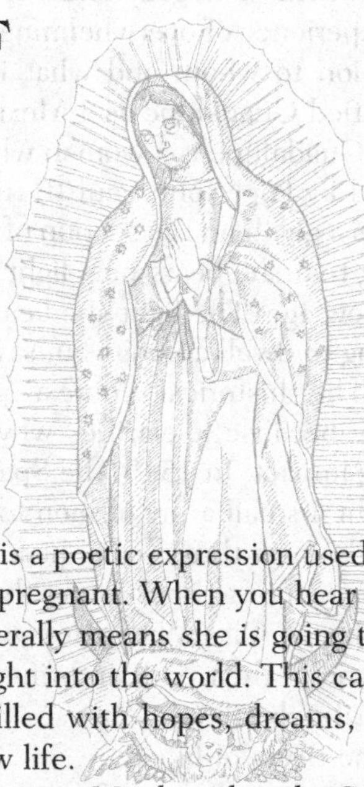

The phrase *dar a luz* (to give light) is a poetic expression used often in Spanish to say that a woman is pregnant. When you hear someone say, "*Ella va a dar a luz*," it literally means she is going to give light. To birth a child is to bring light into the world. This carries a wondrous sense of anticipation, filled with hopes, dreams, angst, worry, yet joy in the coming of new life.

Dar a luz is no isolated expression. Much within the Spanish language and Latino/a culture calls our attention to beginnings, to what is being born. As a child, I remember my grandmother asking me every morning, "*¿Como amaneciste?*" meaning, "how did you awaken?" *Amanecer*, which is both a noun and a verb, can signify dawn, birth, beginnings, and awakening. The Mexican birthday song, *Las Mañanitas*, is sung to the honoree at dawn and bids them to awaken, in effect, to be born again. The song speaks of her/his day of birth as one when many flowers bloomed, when nightingales sang at her/his baptismal font, and when light breaks through darkness to illuminate the coming day. This same song is traditionally sung at dawn to mothers on Mother's Day because they are the bearers of light to the world.

Guadalupe—her image and the account of her apparition—encourages a fascination with birth and with the dawn. In a historical moment of tragedy and hopelessness, the Virgin acknowledges the experience of overwhelming despair, but, nonetheless, calls our attention to whom and what is being born. One historian aptly identified Guadalupe as a Mexican Phoenix.[1]

Guadalupe is a woman who is about to *dar a luz*. Guadalupe, named by Pope John Paul II, the Patroness of all of the Americas, carries a glyph on the section of her robe in front of her womb indicating that she bears new light. Her child in the womb will usher in a new age. The light she bears is the light that is coming. "I am coming to dwell among you, says the Lord."[2]

The historical context preceding the apparition matters greatly because it clarifies why this religious symbol had such a strong impact. In 1519, the Spanish conquistador, Hernán Cortés, brought a small army of men to the shores of Veracruz in Mexico. Over the next three years, he and his army waged war against several indigenous tribes along their route to Tenochtitlan, present-day Mexico City. With gunpowder and horses, they overpowered everyone in their path and finished off the military conquest with a horrific battle in August 1521. The streets of Tenochtitlan became rivers of blood.

The brutality and finality of the conquest, which was a military, political, cultural, and religious defeat, led many indigenous to believe that, as a people, they would cease to exist. Many anticipated being killed off, the few of them remaining enslaved, and their civilization obliterated from the earth. Fundamentally, their gods had failed them, and now they were destined to perish. Not only did many commit suicide, but also some, overcome with despair, ended up killing their newborn children to spare them from a violent and wretched life as slaves. In short, many developed a death wish.

According to the *Nican Mopohua*, in 1531 and ten years after the conquest, a fifty-five-year-old Indio, Juan Diego, started out one cold December morning headed to Tlatelolco, a location within the boundaries of Mexico City. Juan Diego was on his way to daily Mass when he heard beautiful cantos, as if birds were singing. He wondered to himself, *¿Estoy soñando?* ("Am I dreaming?").[3] A beautiful woman appeared before Juan Diego. She was Guadalupe, the source of the poetic cantos. She introduced herself as the "Mother of the God of Great Truth, of Téotl, of the One through Whom We Live, the Creator of Persons, the Owner of What Is Near and Together, of the Lord of Heaven and Earth."[4] She was the one who was going to *dar a luz*.

Guadalupe told Juan Diego to go to Mexico City to Bishop Juan de Zumarraga and tell him that it was her wish that a church be built at Tepeyac, so that she could be present to the recently converted Indios who sought her and who believed in God. In the process, she gave light to a new expression of Christianity. Juan Diego made various attempts to convince Bishop Zumarraga. However, the worldly bishop received Juan Diego's message with a mixture of pastoral sensitivity and skepticism; after all, the bishop surmised, aren't the Indians always having strange visions? And why would the mother of our Lord appear to an Indian? If she were going to appear at all, he reasoned, she would appear to one of the Spaniards who have devoted their lives and fought long and hard for the faith.

Juan Diego returned to Guadalupe shamed by his ineffectiveness with the bishop. Juan Diego suggested to Guadalupe that she send one of the priests with her message. He then explained: "I am one of those *campesinos*, a piece of rope, a small ladder, the excrement of people; I am a leaf; they order me around, lead me by force."[5] What neither the bishop nor Juan Diego understood was that she appeared to give light. She responded by telling Juan Diego that she could send her message with anyone she wished, and she was sending him. On this occasion, she asked him to take a sign from her to Bishop Zumarraga. On the top of Tepeyac hill, Juan Diego gathered roses in his tilma, an apron-like cloth the Indians commonly wore. Guadalupe arranged those roses. Then later, in the presence of Bishop Zumarraga, Juan Diego opened his tilma, allowing the beautiful roses to fall to the floor, revealing the Guadalupe image imprinted on the tilma. Guadalupe gave light and birth to a new church, a newly incarnated faith. This apparition sheds light on the gospel truth of God's enduring presence in our midst, an indigenous truth of *flor y canto*, flower and song.

The miracle of Guadalupe can be found in the apparition's profound recognition of the indigenous approach to truth. We step into the eternal and transcendent through the gift of flower and song. The symbols speak of eternity. In giving light, Guadalupe inspires hope, remains present, and encourages rebirth.

One of the ways Guadalupe gives light is by inspiring hope. The account of Guadalupe takes on much greater import when we consider that the account came into being in the midst of death and destruction. The birth process is one marked by suffering as well as joy. By 1531, the indigenous people of Mexico, and particularly the Aztecs, had suffered a decade as a thoroughly conquered people. The military part of the conquest, which ended in 1521, was marked by the rape of women, the slaughter of indigenous warriors, and the destruction of a way of life. Yet, Guadalupe's brown, mestiza skin color spoke of a life to come, of the birth of a new people. Death would not have the last word. Her very body symbolized the progeny of the mixing of Spanish and indigenous blood. In the midst of overwhelming devastation, hope sprouted forth in the children born from this violent clash. Even today, we are invited to see that hope remains stubbornly insistent in the face of all manner of evil.

Guadalupe gives light in that she promises to remain a faithful presence always. The Guadalupe story is an account of the Holy Spirit's presence to indigenous people and the Spaniards as well. This presence transforms. Both Juan Diego and Bishop Zumarraga came to see themselves differently. Through Guadalupe, light came into spaces and places that had been marked by death in Mesoamerica. In the womb of Mesoamerica, the light of quickening announced the rebirth of the Juan Diegos of this world; that is, the rebirth of those who have known humiliation, but now know their own story of Christian promise. The religious symbolism of Guadalupe proclaims the coming birth of Jesus the Christ in the Americas. In every age, Guadalupe reminds us that Jesus was born, not only in Bethlehem some 2000 years ago, but is always being born anew in our own lives. At one point when Juan Diego is fearful, Guadalupe tells him: "Listen and hear well in your heart, my most abandoned son: that which scares you and troubles you is nothing; do not let your countenance and heart be troubled; do not fear sickness or anxiety. Am I not here, your mother? Are you not under my shadow and my protection? Am I not your source of life? Whom else do you need?"[6] Her faithful presence endures always. Guadalupe invites us into a liminal time and space that encourages rebirth.

It is fitting to celebrate the feast of Guadalupe at a time in which we anticipate the coming light. Her feast, December 12, falls in the midst of Advent. It is a time that marks the end of one liturgical year and the beginning of the next, between the Feast of Christ the King on the last Sunday of the liturgical year and the Sundays of Advent, each marking the coming of new light in the world. She ushers in a new cycle of life, one in which two civilizations, the indigenous and the Spanish, no longer proceed independently of one another but now are interrelated. Accordingly, Guadalupe invites us into liminal space. The children who are the offspring of these two parent civilizations invite their parents into a new space, one in which these two rich cultures and religious beliefs become enriched through their interrelation. Each sees and hears the profundity of God's message of salvation more vividly. While the coming together of the two was violent and brutal, Guadalupe invites both to weave together a new story of the coming light.

May the extraordinary beauty of Guadalupe continue to give light and life to our world.

PRAYER TO THE VIRGIN OF GUADALUPE[7]

Mother of all, you revealed yourself to Juan Diego,
a poor Indian Christian of the Aztec race.

Through his faith and loving cooperation,
You revealed your own and God's love
For all the peoples of the New World,
Both native-American and European.
You promised to answer the cries
Of all who would call upon you at Tepeyac,
Most especially those who were poor
And dispossessed by conquest.
You gave us the marvelous image
Of yourself dressed as an Aztec princess,
Dark-skinned, and pregnant with God's child.

Pray that we might share your tender concern
For all God's children, especially those in need.
And show us the light of your Son both now and always.
Amen.

NOTES

1. D. A. Brading, *Mexican Phoenix: Our Lady of Guadalupe: Image and Tradition Across Five Centuries* (New York: Cambridge University Press, 2003).
2. Zechariah 2:10.
3. Virgil Elizondo, *Guadalupe: Mother of the New Creation* (Maryknoll, NY: Orbis Press, 1997), 6.
4. Ibid., 7–8.
5. Ibid., 10.
6. Ibid., 15–16.
7. Prayer composed by Suzanne Beebe. Used with permission.

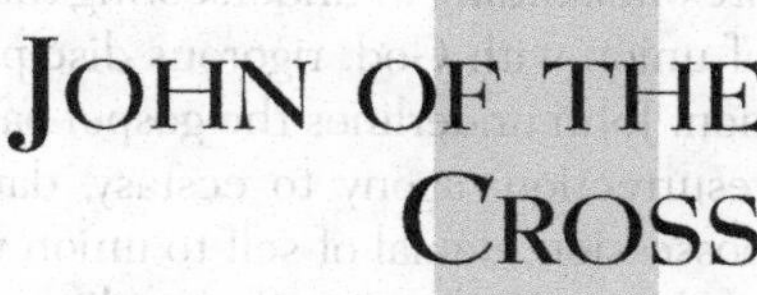

JOHN OF THE CROSS

(1541–1591)

December 14

Born in Spain in 1542, John learned self-sacrificing love from his parents. His father gave up wealth and status when he married a weaver's daughter and was disowned by his noble family. After John's father died, his mother kept the destitute family together as they wandered, homeless, in search of work. John was ordained a Carmelite priest in 1567. John worked with Teresa of Avila for reform, and came to experience its cost.

Many Carmelites felt threatened by this reform, and some members of the order kidnapped him, locked him in a small cell, and beat him three times a week. Yet in that dark and cold desolation, his love and faith were like fire and light. He had nothing left but God. In this death of imprisonment, John came to life, uttering poetry. In the darkness of the dungeon, John's spirit came into the light. John is unique as a mystic-poet, expressing from his prison-cross the ecstasy of mystical union with God. As man-Christian-Carmelite, he experienced this purifying ascent.

As spiritual director, he sensed the holy in others, and as psychologist-theologian, he described it in his writings. His prose works are outstanding in underscoring the cost of discipleship and the path of union with God: rigorous discipline, abandonment, and purification. John underlines the gospel paradox uniquely: the cross leads to resurrection, agony to ecstasy, darkness to light, abandonment to possession, denial of self to union with God. John is a saint because his life was a heroic effort to live up to his name: "of the Cross." In his life, he fully realized the folly of the cross. John composed many works on spiritual growth and prayer that continue to be relevant today: *Ascent of Mount Carmel*, *Dark Night of the Soul*, and *A Spiritual Canticle of the Soul and the Bridegroom Christ*.

JOHN OF THE CROSS

Spiritual Guide and Poet

Thomas Ryan, CSP

The historical context for John's life was sixteenth-century Spain, as it explored the New World and exerted its influence in Europe. John was born in Fondiveros in 1542, the youngest of three brothers. When he was three years old, his father died, leaving the family in financial difficulties. John went to a school for orphans and the poor and worked at a local hospital as a nurse.

John entered the Carmelites at twenty-one and was ordained at twenty-five. His appreciation for silence and solitude led him to think about transferring to the Carthusians, but then he met Teresa of Avila who was initiating a reform movement among Carmelite women's communities. In the year following his ordination and his meeting with Teresa, John and four other Carmelite men opened a reformed house of friars not far from Avila. Taking the name of Friar John of the Cross, he served as master of novices in the new community which identified itself as "discalced" (shoeless), distinguishing it from those Carmelites not entering into the reform who were known as "friars of the observance."[1]

What about John's life is relevant for us today? The inspiration and challenge come from the ability to balance the administrative and the pastoral. Both clergy and laity today are well acquainted with the tension created between attention to administrative and organizational details on the one hand, and availability for service in love to parishioners or family members on the other. Finding a balance between the two, with some personal time worked into the equation as well, is an ongoing challenge for us all.

The wave of expansion within the discalced Carmelites made John a "man on the road." Weighed with building projects, government, spiritual direction, and constant apostolic activity with different groups, he served over the years in various roles—as provincial, as prior, as general definitor (advisor)—with practicality and generosity.

John was what we might today call an active contemplative. He was a man who found intimacy with God in both the hustle and bustle of life and in solitude. What John lifts up for us is that contemplation is alive not only before and after the action, but in the action itself. He managed to achieve a delicate synthesis between solitude and readiness to serve. He knew how to enjoy peace and quiet, and how to let it go when friendship, obedience, or the call to service came knocking.[2]

In his ministry, John traveled an estimated 16,000 miles by foot or on a mule. Can you imagine walking across the United States three times? To travel like an apostle meant bringing a companion with whom he could practice the art of conversation, questioning the other in order to encourage an exchange of thoughts on different questions. And though it was 450 years ago, some things haven't changed: in his travel, lodging, and eating places, he also had to defend himself against thieves and deflect temptations from prostitutes.[3]

In each place, John had his projects: planting and cultivating a garden; building a quarry, aqueduct, or monastery. He absorbed with equanimity the difficulties, displeasure, and annoyances that such extensive projects normally bring in their wake. Witnesses noted the enthusiasm with which he tackled them and the pleasure he derived from them. He mobilized co-workers to carry out the projects, but he was right in the midst of the works with his sleeves rolled up, making bricks and carrying the building materials.

In short, he did not accomplish his building projects only

by prayer and good words while contemplating the countryside. Throughout, his unbreakable triad was fraternity and manual labor, spiritual help and government, contemplation and solitude.[4]

John exhibited true "grace under pressure" in confronting the challenges of the day. The curve balls life throws our way can vary with the individual and season of life, but we all have to face them: health challenges; unemployment; relational breakdowns; financial crises. We need models to inspire us as to how to respond to them, and in John of the Cross, we have one. Rare would be the person who would have to deal with what Friar John had to deal with, and the manner in which he did it is a source of strength for us all.

The Carmel reform in which Teresa and John were engaged was originally supported by the leadership of the Order, albeit with certain restrictions. As the reform moved forward, however, some of the friars of the observance thought it was going too far. John, as a founding member of the first house of the reform, apparently became a target for their upset. In addition, at Teresa's request, John was now serving as a chaplain and confessor for the nuns at the convent of the Incarnation in Avila—a salaried position formerly occupied by the friars of the observance.[5]

John was abducted, taken to a monastery of the observance in Toledo, and imprisoned in a dark, cramped room. As a period of forced inactivity, it was an abrupt break in the rhythm of his dynamic and successful daily activities, and it would last for eight months. He was thirty-five, in the prime of his life, but now stripped of every possibility for work, whether physical, intellectual, or pastoral.

The abductors' goal was to get him to abandon the Teresian reform, to go back on what he had done. Allurements (the office of prior, a more spacious cell with a good library) and punishments (a windowless, nine-foot-long and five-foot-wide, hole-in-the-wall room in which he would be cut off from all communication with others) were the means of pressure used towards this end. Even Teresa did not know what had happened to him.

John began this new period of his life in inner darkness, in need of light and fortitude lest his psychological and spiritual equilibrium be jeopardized for years to come. But God converted the most inactive period in John's life into the most interiorly intense period, transforming it into a time of mystical encounter. Through the poetry John would write in this time of solitude, his "dark night" was converted into a message eventually bringing life and light to a universal audience with deep insights into the ways God can take us to new levels during times of trial.

A few days before escaping by tearing up bed covers into strips and tying them together as his escape rope down to the top of an external monastery wall, he called upon the jailer and asked for his pardon for all the bother and trouble he may have caused him, and offered him his crucifix. Years later, in recalling his sufferings in prison, the norm of interpretation he used was both charitable and compassionate: that those who mistreated him did so because "they thought they were doing the right thing."[6]

John's trials did not stop there. Many examples could be offered, but two salient ones suffice to make the point. Years after his imprisonment, when the reform was in a period of growth and development, one of his confreres, now a prior, undertook to defame him among community members. And the illness that led to his death at forty-nine years of age required painful lancing with scissors and abstraction of pus from abscesses on his shoulder, hip, leg, and foot. His body was so weak that he could not move or turn over in bed; they hung a rope from the ceiling over the bed so that by grasping hold of it he could move a little. Though the suffering was excessive, the infirmarian emphasized his extraordinary patience, the offering he was always making to God of his trials, and his continual thanks to God for favors received.[7]

SPIRITUAL GUIDE AND POET

As shown by the titles of biographies written about him—*God Speaks in the Night* or *When Gods Die*—the core of his teaching about the spiritual life is that the desert periods in our lives are rich with the grace of God if we can only walk in the dark with faith and trust.

Theologically, John was able to see a contradictory and negative reality, whether imprisonment or illness, as endowed with a special beauty and transcendence. One of his oft-quoted lines is: "Where there is no love, put love, and you will draw out love." In the most unfavorable circumstances, he developed an unimaginable creativity. He favored poetry to express his experience of God, and rightfully so, for poetry addresses us at levels of our being where we often are speechless. We have a renewed appreciation today for the power of the human imagination to capture experiences that we can only express imaginatively. For John, imagination was the gate and entry to the soul.

John's most powerful poems are *The Dark Night*, *The Spiritual Canticle*, and *The Living Flame of Love*. Two basic experiences find expression in John's poetry: being wounded and being healed. His major images contain pain: a night in which one is lost (*The Dark Night*); abandonment by a beloved (*The Spiritual Canticle*); a flame that burns (*The Living Flame of Love*). These images reflect an inner experience of being lost, alone, and hurt. They provide us not only with an insight into John's experience but also into our own when we pass through dark valleys and ask, "Where is God in this?" His images have the power to lead us to our own images, and they invite us to engage our creativity in giving expression to our own experience in poetry or paint, music or sculpture.[8]

The language and images John uses in developing his first basic theme—being wounded—can be jolting. But his images of being healed speak of beneficent forces at the heart of reality and lead toward a happy ending. In them we find a reaffirmation of the graciousness of life. The night gives way to dawn. In the words of Carmelite John Welch: "The night in which one was lost becomes a truer guide than the light of noon; the experience of abandonment reveals an unsuspecting presence of the beloved; the painful flame cauterizes, heals, enlivens, bringing warmth and light."[9]

John's commentaries on the poems contained the heart of his teaching and led to his being named a Doctor of the Church, that is, one whose teachings can be taken as a trustworthy guide for our dealings with the yearnings of our hearts and our disordered affections. His poems and his commentary on them point the way to the radical reorientation of desire, to the liberation of an enslaved heart, to the purification of love. His spirituality is particularly apt for adults who are looking for substantive insight into the spiritual journey that anchors and accompanies the process of adult maturation. With the recurring themes of abandonment and divine generosity at its center, John's spirituality challenges us to let go of the known and walk in trust.[10]

In his commentary on *The Living Flame of Love*, John describes where the journey leads: The passions are no longer at war against the will. The appetites seek only what is proper and healthy. One's entire psychic structure is in harmony, operating in accord with the soul's deepest nature and with the God who dwells in its center. And as a result, one lives a harmonious life.

We live in a world today where holistic spirituality is prized and the eastern emphasis on the divine within attracts many followers. In the spirituality of John of the Cross, God is the center of the soul. To be human is to have the capacity for divinization. The paradigm for this experience is the life, death, and resurrection of Jesus Christ. Because of his solidarity with humanity, all authentic human development is now open to participation in divinity, which is, in fact, already in process.[11]

Besides the offices he held, John was the initiator of the Carmelite men's reform, a spiritual master, mystic, poet, and writer. He had been heroic in prison and received the praises of Teresa; he did not want himself to be mythologized and sought to simply live as one more brother among brothers.

What John modeled for us in his living is a precious inheritance: prayer, communion with God in all circumstances, fruitful silence, humility, adaptability, creativity, and attentiveness to the needs of others. These few stanzas from *The Spiritual Canticle* capture something of the mystical song that was his life.

My beloved is the mountains,
and lonely wooded valleys,
strange islands,
and resounding rivers,
the whistling of love-stirring breezes,
the tranquil night
at the time of the rising dawn,
silent music,
sounding solitude,
the supper that refreshes and deepens love.
In the inner wine cellar
I drank of my Beloved, and, when I went abroad
through all this valley
I no longer knew anything,
and lost the herd that I was following.
There He gave me his breast;
there He taught me a sweet and living knowledge;
and I gave myself to Him,
keeping nothing back;
there I promised to be His bride.
Now I occupy my soul
and all my energies in His service;
I no longer tend the herd,
nor have I any other work
now that my every act is love.[12]

A PRAYER WHEN GOD SEEMS FAR AWAY

Saint John of the Cross, in his dark night of the soul, when alone and persecuted, found God and was filled with mystical fire.

O God, your servant, John,
warmed by the grace-filled flame of your love,
became a burning and shining light for your Church.
Help us to have faith that God is for us,
especially when God seems absent and far away.
Grant that we may be enflamed
with the spirit of love and discipline,
and so walk before you as children of radiant light.
We make our prayer through Jesus Christ our Lord. Amen

NOTES

1. John Welch, O.Carm., *When Gods Die: An Introduction to John of the Cross* (New York: Paulist Press, 1990), 3–7.
2. Federico Ruiz, "John of the Cross: A Man of Action," in *God Speaks in the Night: The Life, Times, and Teaching of John of the Cross*, ed. Federico Ruiz (Washington, DC: Institute of Carmelite Studies/ICS Publications, 2000), 258, 259.
3. Jose Vicente Rodriguez, "Apostle and Traveler," in *God Speaks in the Night*, 254–57.
4. Frederico Ruiz, "A Dynamic and Contemplative Man," in *God Speaks in the Night*, 323.
5. Welch, *When Gods Die*, 9–10.
6. Frederico Ruiz, "Night and Dawn: Transfiguration in Toledo," in *God Speaks in the Night*, 158–67.
7. Jose Vicente Rodriguez, "Death and Glorification," in *God Speaks in the Night*, 365.
8. Welch, *When Gods Die*, 19–20, 29.
9. Ibid., 20.
10. Ibid., 2.

11. Ibid., 64.

12. John of the Cross, "The Spiritual Canticle," stanzas 14, 15, 26, 27, 28, in *The Collected Works of St. John of the Cross*, trans. Kieran Kavanaugh, OCD, Otilio Rodriguez, OCD (Washington, DC: Institute of Carmelite Studies/ICS Publications, 1991), 473, 475. John's poem "The Spiritual Canticle" was written during his imprisonment, in confined, dark, and cramped conditions, beset with foul odors, "in a tomb." But it is described as "the poem with the greatest feel for open space, countrysides, movement and fragrance that exists in Spanish poetry. There is more than a poetic escape. What one has is a prayer, a mystical song." Federico Ruiz, *God Speaks in the Night*, 172.

Isaac Thomas Hecker

(1819–1888)

December 22

Isaac Thomas Hecker was born in New York City on December 18, 1819. Ordained a Redemptorist priest in 1849, he founded the Missionary Society of St. Paul the Apostle in New York in 1858. The society was established to evangelize both believers and non-believers in order to convert North America to the Roman Catholic Church. Father Hecker sought to evangelize Americans using the popular means of his day, primarily preaching, the public lecture circuit, and the printing press. He founded the monthly publication *The Catholic World* in 1865. Hecker's spirituality centered on the action of the Holy Spirit upon the soul and the need to remain attentive to the prompting of the Spirit in the great and small moments of life. Under the guidance of the Holy Spirit, Father Hecker labored to establish a dialogue between faith and culture, which he believed would lead to an American Catholicism whose vitality and optimism would transform the world. In the latter years of his life, Father Hecker suffered dark nights of the soul that varied in intensity. While emotionally and physically overcome at moments, Father Hecker remained firm in his sure belief in the Holy Spirit. On December 22, 1888, as the Paulist community gathered around his bed in prayer, Father Hecker raised his hand, making the Sign of the Cross in blessing, and died. In 2009, Isaac Thomas Hecker was declared Servant of God, and his cause for sainthood began.

ISAAC THOMAS HECKER

Servant of God

Ronald A. Franco, CSP

Servant of God Isaac Hecker's life unfolded against the background of a dynamic modern American society in constant transition. His younger years, culminating in his baptism as a Roman Catholic in 1844, were a period of intense spiritual seeking. As an enthusiastic new Catholic, missionary priest, and author, Hecker's spiritual search was transformed into an evangelizing energy, which found fulfillment in the period of his most comprehensive pastoral and missionary activity that began with the founding of the Paulist Fathers in 1858. In his final years until his death in 1888, Hecker's spiritual doctrine and missionary zeal matured and deepened in a context of debilitating illness and personal suffering. Through it all, his lifelong spiritual journey highlighted the distinctive action of God's grace illuminating the holiness of his life for the building up of the Church. His life story, spiritual journey, and missionary zeal remain especially significant and relevant for the Church today.

Not unlike America in the twenty-first century, the United States in the nineteenth century was a diverse religious marketplace in which individuals could freely choose whatever religion seemed to suit them. Then, as now, there was a considerable amount of movement by Americans from one religious group to another. By his own account, the young Isaac Hecker examined the principal Protestant sects, sampling as many as possible of the leading contemporary religious ideas, from Methodism to Unitarianism, and participating in utopian experiments in community life. Somewhat to his own surprise, he finally found what he had been looking for in Roman Catholicism, whose doctrine of the Communion of Saints had especially impressed him.

Like Christian history's most famous seeker, Saint Augustine, Hecker eloquently exemplifies the spiritual search in its most intense form. Like Augustine, Hecker engaged the leading intellectual and religious currents of his time, before finally finding his permanent religious home in the Roman Catholic Church. The very personal story of his spiritual search, of his intense attention to his own inner spiritual sense, certainly speaks to the spiritual longings of our own spiritually hungry century, with its growing number of those claiming to be "spiritual but not religious."

The young Hecker was also, in a certain sense, "spiritual but not religious" for most of the first twenty-five years of his life. Significantly, however, he did not remain that way. For Hecker, the spiritual search was never an end in itself. The point of seeking was to find. Once the object was found, the search ceased; or, more precisely, was transformed into commitment and action.

Hecker found fulfillment in the Catholic Church. He never either regretted what he had found or desired to look further, but rather devoted the rest of his life to helping other seekers to find the truth in the Catholic Church. After his conversion, all his activity was characterized by an enthusiastic embrace of the Church. His earnest personal spiritual search had led him to the Church and would transform him into its committed missionary. Hecker's enthusiasm for his new faith and his commitment to the Church permeate all his subsequent activity and writing, both before and after the founding of the Paulists.

Fundamental to the young Hecker's spiritual experience had been his recognition of the indwelling Holy Spirit of God acting in and through the questions of his soul to call him out of himself and into the Church. In thus interpreting and universalizing his own spiritual quest, Hecker emphasized what would become his lifelong conviction: that Catholicism was consistent with and indeed the true fulfillment of the aspirations of human nature. This conjures up a nineteenth-century retrieval of the theme of St. Augustine's *Confessions*: "You have made us for yourself, O Lord, and our heart is restless until it rests in you."[1]

The sanctity most specifically characteristic of Hecker's spiritual search can be recognized in his recognition of God's providential presence and action in his life and in his personal response to the presence and action of the Holy Spirit. That experience of God informed his enthusiastic embrace of the Church and facilitated a life of active, priestly ministry, first as a Redemptorist and then later as the founder of the Paulist Fathers. This intense personal commitment to the Church as the institutional expression of the presence and providential action of the Holy Spirit in the world would sustain him throughout his ministry and through the difficult experiences and challenges that punctuated it.

Hecker spent his Redemptorist years largely in parish missions, a type of parish renewal experience intended to elevate the spiritual life of the faithful and to bring back to the sacraments those who had lapsed or become alienated. By challenging Catholics to a higher standard of moral behavior (for example, by reducing alcohol abuse), the missions, in Hecker's view, contributed to improving the quality of Catholic life. He hoped this approach would make the Church more attractive to non-Catholics. Hecker quickly came to recognize that any successful mission to non-Catholic America required an effective mission and ministry within the American Catholic community, and vice versa. For the rest of his life, Hecker would repeatedly emphasize this reciprocal relationship between the mission within and to the Catholic community and the mission outward to the larger American society.

Looking back on Hecker's ideas from the vantage point of the Church and the call for a "New Evangelization," we can especially appreciate his commitment to challenge American Catholics to the fullness of their mission: to evangelize society and to enhance the quality of Church life by building up the Catholic Church in the United States.

> We cannot even preserve the faith among Catholics in any better way than by advancing it among our non-Catholic brethren. Indeed, simply to preserve the faith it is necessary to extend it. It is a state of chronic disease for men to live together and not endeavor to communicate their respective good fortune. A Catholic without a mission to his non-Catholic fellow-citizens in these times, and when only a small portion of the human race has the true religion, is only half a Catholic.[2]

The nineteenth-century Paulists' emphases on liturgy and preaching in their New York parish clearly exemplified that commitment to the qualitative enhancement of American Catholic communal life. We are even more apt to appreciate today the importance of internal Church community life for the effectiveness of its mission outward to society.

In his preaching and writing, Isaac Hecker self-consciously sought and promoted images and models of holiness that he believed resonated well within the new context created by what he saw happening in the modern world. Hence, Hecker was constantly preoccupied with making viable connections between Roman Catholicism and modern American values and institutions. Far from being a call for conformity to secular culture, this was a definite evangelizing strategy for Hecker. He was convinced that the same Holy Spirit who spoke in his own heart and in human hearts in general also spoke through the Church. The evangelization of American society through missionary action aimed at the conversion of individuals would benefit both Church and civil society.

Like Alexis de Tocqueville (1805–1859), the famous nineteenth-century observer, Hecker appreciated the problem posed by the fundamentally fragmented character of modern democratic society. Hecker understood the tenuous and fragile connections between individuals, and the dilemma of how to create a modern community that unites individuals in a way that is consistent with democratic customs and a culture of freedom.

In nineteenth-century Europe, where the Church was struggling to survive as an institution against an overtly hostile, liberal political order, it sought to counteract the social fragmentation associated with liberalism. It sought to reconnect increasingly isolated individuals into a community by preserving, repairing, or restoring traditional religious bonds. One way to do this was to assert the Church's claims to authority as vigorously as possible and to insist upon its traditional privileges and institutional rights in relation to the state. In contrast to that European political approach, Hecker's American alternative saw a social solution, in which individuals were converted to and transformed by Catholicism as the answer to their deepest human aspirations. By being open to the outpouring of the Holy Spirit in their own lives, Americans would be empowered to exercise their democratic liberty consistent with the truth contained in Catholicism.

At his very first audience with Blessed Pope Pius IX in 1857, in response to the Pope's concern about factional strife in the United States, Hecker confidently replied that the effect of Catholic truth on a society torn by partisan division would be "like oil on troubled waters."[3] Some thirty years later, in one of his last *Catholic World* articles published in the year he died, Hecker quoted an anonymous acquaintance to the effect that "he didn't care for union of church and state if he could have union of church and people."[4] Such comments convey how important the transformation of society through the conversion of individuals was for Hecker, and how he confidently expected this to accomplish what, prior to his conversion, he had once imagined might be accomplished through political activity and social reform.

Having experienced the divided and fragmented character of so much of contemporary American religion, Hecker appreciated the importance of authority in the Church as the divinely sanctioned providential alternative to the principle of individual interpretation. For Hecker, the internal order of the visible institutional Church was the divinely ordained means for the fulfillment of Christ's life and mission on earth, pouring the oil of the Holy Spirit on the troubled waters of the world. Through the Church and its sacraments and worship, people would be brought into direct contact with Christ. Thus sanctified, they would be transformed by the power of the Holy Spirit, present and active within them.

Hecker's uncompromising affirmation of Church authority and his equally uncompromising commitment to the purpose for that authority speak directly to our even more religiously and culturally fragmented time. The Church is constantly being challenged not just to proclaim its authoritative answers, but also to incarnate a communal experience of the Body of Christ in the world, as people continue to search both outside and inside the Church.

Although Hecker remained both Paulist General Superior and parish pastor from 1858 through his death in 1888, the last years of his life were dominated by physical illness and suffering. Sickness and suffering are complex human experiences that elicit different reactions and responses in each of us. In Hecker's case, unwanted sickness and suffering served to help his final spiritual maturation in response to God's grace. His sickness deepened his relationship with the Lord and broadened his evangelizing zeal, even as his apostolic activity was curtailed. Indeed, his illness intensely focused Hecker on the one most important thing: his personal relationship with God, which imparts ultimate meaning and importance to what one does with one's life.

In the first stage of his life, Hecker was animated by a conscious appreciation of God's providence and allowed himself to be guided by the Holy Spirit. He discerned the divine presence in God's lifelong providential care for him, through which he received the grace to follow the Roman Catholic Church. In the second stage of his life, his enthusiastic embrace of the Church had led him to an active vocation as a priest and religious and formed him into a thoroughly committed churchman. He was thus well-prepared and spiritually equipped for his period of active Paulist mission and leadership, during which he concentrated on the Church's essential mission of evangelization, both within the Church and outward to the world.

He planted his vision in the solid soil of the first American men's religious community and its growing New York parish. He expanded a network of preaching missions, lecturing, and publishing. Finally, at the end of his life, immersed in his own dark night of the soul, he surrendered himself and all his activities to the call to conform his life to the mystery of Christ's Cross—in the words of his patron, St. Paul, "*filling up what is lacking in the afflictions of Christ, on behalf of his body, which is the church*."[5]

Through it all, Hecker lived in hope—hope in that truth that would answer people's deepest questions and loftiest aspirations and that would heal and reconcile the contentious divisions and alienation of a modern society.

Ever since the Apostles, evangelization happens when people are excited enough about the Gospel story to proclaim it and when they really believe that those they tell it to will be better off—both individually and as a society—because of it. In a politically polarized and socially fragmented society, in which so much of what had been taken for granted was now up for grabs, Hecker affirmed the action of the Holy Spirit responding to contemporary questions and aspirations. What he experienced in his own personal quest, he then modeled in his ministry as a priest, pastor, and religious founder, proclaiming Catholic faith and building Catholic community.

Witnessing to the good news Christ has entrusted to his Church is the unchangingly permanent and essential mission of the Church in every time and place. As the term "new evangelization" suggests, changing circumstances pose new challenges. Some, such as the modern search for spiritual meaning in a materialistic culture, would have seemed very familiar to Hecker and his contemporaries. Some, such as religion's radically reduced presence in public culture and recent social and political realignments within American religions, would likely have surprised him. Expected or unexpected, these challenges all require what Hecker called "presenting the same old truths in new forms, fresh new tone and air and spirit."[6] Today's true task is to imagine how Hecker's life story, spiritual journey, Catholic zeal, and heroic sanctity may inspire and motivate American Catholics to respond with equivalent energy to the heightened challenges of the twenty-first century.

PRAYER FOR THE INTERCESSION OF SERVANT OF GOD ISAAC THOMAS HECKER[7]

Heavenly Father, you called servant of God,
Isaac Thomas Hecker,
to preach the Gospel to the people of North America
and through his teaching,
to know the peace and the power
of your indwelling Spirit.
He walked in the footsteps of Saint Paul the Apostle,
and like Paul spoke your Word with a zeal for souls
and a burning love for all who came to him in need.

Look upon us this day with compassion and hope
and hear our prayer.
We ask that through the intercession of Father Hecker,
your servant, you might answer our prayers.
We ask this in the name of Jesus Christ, Your Son, Our Lord,
who lives and reigns with You and the Holy Spirit,
one God, forever and ever. Amen

NOTES

1. Augustine, *Confessions*, I, i.

2. "The Human Environments of the Catholic Faith," *The Catholic World*, July 1886, 468.

3. "From a letter to the American Fathers, dated Rome, December 22, 1857," *The Paulist Vocation*, 46.

4. "The Mission of Leo XIII," *Catholic World*, 48, 1888, 9.

5. Colossians 1:24.

6. "Personal Sanctification of the Paulist and His Standard of Perfection," *The Paulist Vocation*, 125.

7. Paulist Fathers' Office for the Cause of Isaac Thomas Hecker.

ADDITIONAL READING

Behl, Vincent Ferrer, SJ. *Pilgrim Journey: John Henry Newman 1801–1845*. Mahwah: Paulist Press, 2001.

Branch, Taylor. *Parting the Waters: America in the King Years 1954–1964*. New York: Simon and Schuster, 1988.

Burke, Kevin F., and Eileen Burke-Sullivan. *The Ignatian Tradition*. Collegeville, MN: Liturgical Press, 2009.

Day, Dorothy. *The Long Loneliness*. New York: Harper, 1952.

DeLaura, David, ed. *John Henry Newman, Apologia Pro Vita Sua*. New York: Norton, 1968.

Delio, Ilia. *Franciscan Prayer*. Cincinnati, OH: St. Anthony Messenger Press, 2004.

Kelly, Ellin, and Annabelle Melville, eds. *Elizabeth Seton: Selected Writings*. New York: Paulist Press, 1987.

Murphy-O'Connor, Jerome. *Paul: His Story*. Oxford, 2004.

Payne, Steven, OCD, ed. *John of the Cross: Conferences and Essays by Members of the Institute of Carmelite Studies*. Washington, DC: ICS Publications, 1992.

Philippe, Marie-Dominque, OP. *The Mystery of Joseph*. San Francisco: Ignatius Press, 2005.

Pope John XXIII. *Journal of a Soul*. Translated by Dorothy White. Garden City: Image Books/Doubleday, 1980.

Turks, Paul, of the Oratory. *Philip Neri: The Fire of Joy*. New York: Alba House, 1995.

Vauchez, André. *Francis of Assisi: The Life and Afterlife of a Medieval Saint*. Translated by Michael F. Cusato. New Haven, CT: Yale University Press, 2012.

Vigil, María López. *Oscar Romero: Memories in Mosaic*. Translated by Kathy Ogle. Washington, DC: EPICA, 2000.

Williams, Rowan. *Teresa of Avila*. London; New York: Continuum, 2004.

CONTRIBUTORS

DIANE APOSTOLOS-CAPPADONA is Visiting Professor of Religious Art and Cultural History in the Catholic Studies Program and Women's & Gender Studies Program at Georgetown University. Among her many publications are essays in academic journals, conference volumes, and thematic collections about biblical women such as Judith, Salome, Haemorrhissa, Mary of Nazareth, and Mary Magdalene. She is the author of *In Search of Mary Magdalene: Images and Traditions* (2002) and is currently completing *Christian Art: A Companion Guide* (2014).

SUZANNE BEEBE is currently a graduate student at Boston College School of Theology and Ministry, writing faith-based dramatic pieces that explore religious issues for catechetical purposes. In the past she has worked in city government, Catholic journalism (as associate editor at St. Anthony Messenger Publications), high-tech marketing communications, and religious education programs in the Boston Archdiocese.

FRANCINE CARDMAN teaches Historical Theology and Church History at Boston College School of Theology and Ministry. She publishes and lectures on the development of early Christian ethics, women's ministry and leadership, and the history of Christian spirituality.

JOHN E. COLLINS, a native New Yorker, was ordained a Paulist priest in 1970. Since then he has been active in parish and campus ministry throughout the country. He was Diocesan Director of Campus Ministry and Director of the Catholic Student Center at The Ohio State University in Columbus, Ohio. Over the past two decades, Fr. Collins has conducted more than four hundred missions and preached over thirty retreats for priests and religious. He presently devotes his full-time energies to evangelization and mission work from his home parish, St. Paul the Apostle Church on the west side of New York City.

PAULA CUOZZO, a Paulist Associate, earned a Master's in Theological Studies from Weston Jesuit School of Theology in Cambridge, MA, with a dual concentration in Systematics and Spirituality. Her Master's thesis examined the role of the Holy Spirit and Church authority in the works of Isaac Hecker, founder of the Paulists. She currently serves as the Director of the RCIA program at the Paulist Center in Boston.

MARY R. D'ANGELO teaches in the Department of Theology and in the Gender Studies Program at the University of Notre Dame, specializing in New Testament and Christian Origins. With Ross Kraemer, she edited *Women and Christian Origins* from Oxford University Press. She has also published numerous articles on women, gender, imperial politics, theological language, and sexual practice in early Christianity.

ANNE DENEEN is a full-time Lutheran pastor, serving in Gloucester, Massachusetts. A graduate of Weston Jesuit School of Theology, she is also a spiritual director to many people on the north shore of Boston. Dietrich Bonhoeffer's life and work have been formative for her theology and her pastoral practice. Lutherans all over the world honor Bonhoeffer for his life, his theological and political witness, and his martyrdom.

FRANK DESIANO was ordained a Paulist priest in 1972 and has served in downtown parishes in New York and Chicago. He earned a D.Min. from Boston University in 1990 on the topic of "Parish Based Evangelization." A widely known speaker to clergy and catechists, he also directs parish renewal across the country. He has written numerous books, notably *Mission America: Challenges and Obstacles for Catholics Today*, and an e-book on the Synod, 2012 (Paulist Press). He presently lives in Washington, DC.

DOMINIC F. DOYLE is an Associate Professor in Systematic Theology at Boston College School of Theology and Ministry. He was born in London, England, and holds a B.A. in Theology and Religious Studies from the University of Cambridge, an M.T.S. from Harvard Divinity School, and a Ph.D. from Boston College. His interests include theological anthropology, theology of culture, and the doctrine of God, with a particular interest in Thomas Aquinas and Karl Rahner.

LEWIS S. FIORELLI is an Oblate of St. Francis de Sales who currently serves in a northern Virginia parish. Formerly Superior General of the Oblate Congregation, he taught dogmatic theology and Salesian spirituality in Washington, DC. A noted spiritual guide and retreat director, he has worked extensively with lay Salesian groups as well as with the monasteries of the Visitation of Holy Mary in the United States. Recent writings include: "Winning Hearts: Ministering in a Salesian Manner," in *Human Encounter in the Salesian Tradition and Inspired Common Sense: Seven Fundamental Themes of Salesian Spirituality*.

RONALD A. FRANCO, a native of New York City, entered the Paulist Fathers in 1981 and was ordained a priest in 1995. He is Vice-Postulator for the canonization cause of Paulist Founder Isaac Thomas Hecker. He has served in Toronto and New York. Since 2010, he has been pastor of the historic Immaculate Conception Church in Knoxville, Tennessee.

COLLEEN M. GRIFFITH is Associate Professor of the Practice of Theology at Boston College School of Theology and Ministry. Working at the intersection of theology and spirituality, her writing and research interests focus in the areas of theological anthropology, historical and contemporary spirituality, and theological method. Her most recent publications include *Catholic Spiritual Practices: A Treasury of Old and New* edited with Thomas H. Groome, and *Prophetic Witness: Catholic Women's Strategies for Reform*, for which she received a first-place award from the Catholic Press Association.

MARGARET ELETTA GUIDER is a member of the Sisters of St. Francis of Mary Immaculate (Joliet, IL) and recently concluded four years in congregation leadership. As Associate Professor of Missiology at the Boston College School of Theology and Ministry, her teaching and research interests focus on ecclesiology, Mariology, consecrated life and the interdisciplinary study of religion and culture. Sr. Guider is past president of the American Society of Missiology and serves as consultant to religious institutes, missionary societies, and faith-based institutions.

BRETT C. HOOVER is an assistant professor in the Department of Theological Studies at Loyola Marymount University in Los Angeles. He is the author of *Comfort: An Atlas for the Body and Soul* (New York: Riverhead, 2012). His book on multicultural Catholic parishes, *The Shared Parish: Latinos, Euro-Americans, and the Future of U.S. Catholicism* will be published by New York University Press in 2014.

THOMAS A. KANE teaches Pastoral Studies at Boston College School of Theology and Ministry in Chestnut Hill, MA, and directs Paulist Reconciliation Ministries in Washington, DC. He is the editor of a new collection of essays, *Healing God's People, A Reconciliation Reader* and the revised *Landings* program for returning Catholics, both published by Paulist Press. He is an internationally known ritual maker and videographer and studies contemporary celebration. He has written and lectured on liturgy, dance, and creativity in the United States and abroad.

MICHAEL MCGARRY is a Paulist priest, who has served at the University of Texas, Boston's Paulist Center, St. Paul's College (Washington, DC), and at the University of California at Berkeley. With a specialty in Jewish-Christian relations, he was Rector of the Tantur Ecumenical Institute in Jerusalem for eleven years. From 2010–2014, he served as president for the Paulist Fathers in Queens, NY. He is author of *Christology after Auschwitz*, and co-author of *Pope John Paul II in the Holy Land* and *Pope Benedict XVI in the Holy Land* (all Paulist Press).

CATHERINE M. MOONEY is an associate professor of church history at Boston College School of Theology and Ministry. Her research focuses on Christian saints and spirituality. Her publications include *Gendered Voices: Medieval Saints and Their Interpreters*; *Philippine Duchesne: A Woman with the Poor*; a book forthcoming from the University of Pennsylvania Press on Clare of Assisi; and essays on the medieval church, Ignatian spirituality, and saints, such as Francis of Assisi, Angela of Foligno, Catherine of Siena, and Teresa of Avila.

D. BRUCE NIELI is a full-time Paulist evangelist and missionary, working in the South, especially Tennessee and Texas. He served for seven years at St. Paul the Apostle Church on Manhattan's West Side. He is the founding director of the Center for Spiritual Development in the Archdiocese of New York, the founding Director of Evangelization, Texas Catholic Conference, and served as Director for Evangelization for United States Conference of Catholic Bishops.

NANCY PINEDA-MADRID is Associate Professor of Theology and Latina/o Ministry at Boston College School of Theology and Ministry. She holds a Ph.D. in Systematic and Philosophical Theology from the Graduate Theological Union. In 2011, she published the book, *Suffering and Salvation in Ciudad Juárez*, and in 2013, she co-edited the book, *Hope: Promise, Possibility, and Fulfillment*. Currently, she is working on a book on Our Lady of Guadalupe. In 2012, the Sisters of Loretto honored her with their Loretto Legacy Award for Religion and Theology.

JAMES F. PUGLISI is the Minister General of the Franciscan Friars of the Atonement and Director of the Ecumenical Research Center, *Centro Pro Unione*, Rome, Italy. He is Professor of Ecclesiology, Ecumenism and Sacraments at the Pontifical Ateneo Sant'Anselmo and Director of the department of Ecumenical and Interreligious Studies at the Pontifical University of St. Thomas, Angelicum. He has been member of several international ecumenical dialogues for the Pontifical Council for the Promotion of Christian Unity and Faith and Order Commission of the World Council of Churches.

PAUL GERARD ROBICHAUD is the historian of the Paulist Fathers and the Postulator for the Cause of Isaac Thomas Hecker, CSP. He has a doctorate in American Intellectual and Cultural History from the University of California, Los Angeles, and he has taught in the history department at the Catholic University of America. He has also served as Rector of the Church of Santa Susanna in Rome and as General Secretary of the American Catholic Historical Society.

THOMAS RYAN is a Paulist priest who has served in campus ministry at Ohio State University in Columbus and McGill University in Montreal; directed the Canadian Centre for Ecumenism; served as co-founder and director of *Unitas*, an ecumenical center for spirituality in Montreal, and as founder-director of the Paulist North American Office for Ecumenical and Interfaith Relations in Washington, DC. He leads retreats and preaches parish missions throughout North America and is the author of fourteen books relating to spirituality.

JOHN RANDALL SACHS, Associate Professor of Systematic Theology at the Boston College School of Theology and Ministry, has been a Jesuit for over forty years. He is the author of articles on Ignatian and creation spirituality and is actively giving Ignatian retreats and spiritual direction.

THOMAS STEGMAN is a Wisconsin Province Jesuit who teaches New Testament at Boston College School of Theology and Ministry in Chestnut Hill, MA. He is the author of *The Character of Jesus: The Linchpin to Paul's Argument in 2 Corinthians* (Pontifical Biblical Institute) and *Second Corinthians* (Baker Academic), part of the Catholic Commentary on Sacred Scripture series. While his scholarly interests focus mostly on the Pauline corpus, Fr. Stegman also writes on pastoral and liturgical implications of New Testament texts.

O. Ernesto Valiente received his PhD from the University of Notre Dame and is assistant professor of systematic theology at Boston College School of Theology and Ministry. He is currently working on a monograph entitled *Following Jesus from Conflict to Communion: A Liberationist Approach to Reconciliation*. Ernesto lives with his wife and daughter in Watertown, MA.

James A. Wallace is a Redemptorist priest who taught homiletics at the Washington Theological Union (1986–2012), before becoming director of San Alfonso Retreat House in Long Branch, NJ in 2013. His publications include *Preaching to the Hungers of the Heart: The Homily on the Feasts and Within the Rites*, *The Ministry of Lector*, and *Lift Up Your Hearts, Homilies for Cycles A, B, and C*, with Robert P. Waznak and Guerric DeBona, OSB. He has given workshops and conferences, parish missions and retreats in the USA and abroad.